The Cambridge Manuals of Science and
Literature

T0352338

THE MORAL LIFE
AND MORAL WORTH

THE
MORAL LIFE
AND MORAL WORTH

BY

W. R. SORLEY

LITT.D., HON. LL.D. EDIN., F.B.A.
KNIGHTBRIDGE PROFESSOR
OF MORAL PHILOSOPHY

Cambridge:
at the University Press
1930

CAMBRIDGE UNIVERSITY PRESS
Cambridge, New York, Melbourne, Madrid, Cape Town,
Singapore, São Paulo, Delhi, Tokyo, Mexico City

Cambridge University Press
The Edinburgh Building, Cambridge CB2 8RU, UK

Published in the United States of America by Cambridge University Press, New York

www.cambridge.org
Information on this title: www.cambridge.org/9781107605879

First Edition, 1911
Second Edition, 1913
Third Edition, 1920
Reprinted, 1930
First paperback edition 2011

A catalogue record for this publication is available from the British Library

ISBN 978-1-107-60587-9 Paperback

*With the exception of the coat of arms at
the foot, the design on the title page is a
reproduction of one used by the earliest known
Cambridge printer, John Siberch,* **1521**

PREFATORY NOTE

THE purpose of the following pages is to give a popular account of the nature of goodness in human life. They are not specially addressed to the philosophical student, but to the wider public interested in the subject: for moral philosophy is the quest of a few, but morality is every man's affair. Nor is the book an essay in casuistry. Cases of conduct are infinite in number, and hardly two of them are the same; general rules fit them awkwardly. But morality is a spirit manifested in life, not a body of rules; and this point of view is marked by the title *The Moral Life*.

W. R. S.

September 1911.

First Edition, 1911
Second Edition, 1913
Third Edition, 1920
Reprinted, 1930

CONTENTS

THE MORAL LIFE

AND MORAL WORTH

CHAPTER I

Two questions, distinct from one another in kind, may be asked about the moral life. One of these is a question of fact and history, the other is a question of validity or of worth. The conduct of man is distinguished from the behaviour of animals by the presence of moral ideas. These ideas appear in the way in which he regards conduct and the character which issues in conduct : some things are approved by him and called good ; others he disapproves and calls bad. When we inquire into the origin of moral ideas, or trace their connexion with the physical and social environment, or follow the stages in their development from their earliest to their present form, we are occupied with the historical question. But behind this question lies another of equal or greater interest. The historian may be able to tell us what kind of life was held to be good at any time, and how the ideas about the

A

good life have varied or developed ; but when he goes on to say whether the life called good was really good or not, he is no longer a mere historian ; he has raised the question of the validity of the ideas which he records, and of the worth of the life which he describes. In doing so he has passed to a new point of view, which is not that of the historian but that of the moralist. It is from this latter point of view that the moral life will be regarded in the following pages. Their purpose is to give an account of the characteristics of human life which are good or praiseworthy and which are commonly described by the term virtue.

With the history of morality we are not directly concerned ; but a few sentences on its method and results will lead up to the consideration of the moral life from the point of view of its value or worth. The varieties of moral conduct and moral codes have long been a commonplace of reflective writers. The differences are not merely in modes of conduct ; they affect the ideas and judgments of men. One race or one age condemns what has been approved by another. " There is nothing just or unjust," said Pascal, " which does not change its quality with a change of climate. Three degrees of latitude over-turn the whole science of law." The qualities most admired are those that suit the circumstances of a people. Where war is the common business,

courage is accounted the chief among the virtues ;
a settled society looks for justice in the social order ;
in the industrial state honesty and straightforward
dealing are praised and approved, even by those who
do not practise them. There is a similar variety in
the faults which are condoned. In the words of
Macaulay, " Every age and every nation has certain
characteristic vices, which prevail almost universally,
which scarcely any person scruples to avow, and
which even rigid moralists but faintly censure.
Succeeding generations change the fashion of their
morals with the fashion of their hats and their
coaches, take some other kind of wickedness under
their patronage, and wonder at the depravity of
their ancestors."

The remarks of Pascal and Macaulay are merely
illustrations of a view expressed by many writers in
different periods. They observe the varieties of
moral ideas, and occasionally hint at a cause for the
variation. With Pascal it is climate ; Macaulay
speaks of it as a mere fashion. There is no attempt
to bring all the facts together and look at the process
as a whole. To do this has been the work of quite
recent times. Great stores of knowledge have been
accumulated regarding the customs and ideas of races,
civilised and uncivilised, and the theory of evolu-
tion has put into our hands a clue for understanding
this material. In this way a scientific history of

morals has arisen. Much still remains matter of conjecture ; but it is possible to state certain results with a fair degree of confidence.

In the first place, we are able to affirm that, so far as our evidence goes, morality in some form has always been a factor in human life. Men are never without some consciousness of a distinction between good and evil, between things that are to be done and things that are to be avoided. This conclusion has been disputed, it is true, but only because too narrow an interpretation has been put upon morality. The savage may not have the same abstract notions as the civilised man, and he may approve what the latter condemns, but he is not therefore without a conscience. A single case will illustrate the point : " Mr Howitt once said to a young Australian native with whom he was speaking about the food prohibited during initiation, ' But if you were hungry and caught a female opossum, you might eat it if the old men were not there.' The youth replied, ' I could not do that ; it would not be right ' ; and he could give no other reason than that it would be wrong to disregard the customs of his people." The particular prohibition has nothing to do with morality, as the civilised man understands morality, but to the savage it was a moral prohibition, which his conscience enforced, irrespective of any actual command or probable penalty : " the customs of

his people " were for him the measure of right and
wrong.

This points to a second conclusion which may be
drawn from the historical study of morality. In
early societies there is no distinction between custom
and morality ; the customs of the tribe are reflected
in the individual conscience, and exercise a regulating
influence upon individual conduct.   Nor is there any
law or any morality outside this customary rule.
Every part of it tends to have the same sanctity for
members of the tribe.   There are no defined punish-
ments for disobedience ; but breach of the most trivial
rules may be visited with the severest consequences.
When some of these customary requirements are
laid down as positive commands and enforced by
penalties for nonconformity, law is beginning to
take an independent position ; when portions of it
are regarded as authoritative for their own sake and
not simply because they are customary, morality
and custom are coming to be distinguished.   But
in the beginning these distinctions did not exist.   In
the tribal stage of society men show little independence of character, and they are not given to reflection.
They are social—or tribal—to the core ; " they
think in herds " ; and they follow the tradition of the
tribe as their rule of right and wrong.

We enter more debatable ground if we seek, in
the third place, to estimate the amount of difference

that actually exists, or has existed, between the moral codes of different communities. The great diversity of moral ideas is the thing that strikes one first and most forcibly. Cruelty, intemperance, cowardice, untruthfulness, disregard of human life, have all been practised, at one time or another, by one people or another, without remorse and without rebuke. Perhaps there is no precept of the moral law that could stand the old test of universal assent —" always, everywhere, and by all men." These things cannot be explained away. At the same time they are only one part of the story of morality. It is easy to magnify the differences. Vices may be acquiesced in without being held to be virtues. The coward may still admire bravery, the liar truth, the intemperate man self-restraint, although he condones his own lack of the virtue. Further, we must remember that early morality is tribal morality ; to understand the moral attitude of the members of a tribe, we must look to the conduct which they approve between man and man within the tribe, and not to their behaviour towards strangers or enemies. Looking from this point of view, Dr Westermarck sums up the results of his inquiry into the history of moral ideas in the following words : " When we examine the moral rules of uncivilised races we find that they in a very large measure resemble those prevalent among nations of culture. In every savage community homicide is prohibited by custom, and so is theft. Savages also regard charity as a duty and praise generosity as a virtue—indeed, their customs concerning mutual aid are often much more stringent than our own ; and many uncivilised peoples are conspicuous for their aversion to telling lies. But at the same time," he goes on to add, " there is a considerable difference between the regard for life, property, truth, and the general well-being of a neighbour, which displays itself in primitive rules of morality and that which is found among ourselves."

Perhaps it is not too much to say that the whole difference results from the primitive identification of morality with tribal custom. The progress of moral ideas depends upon their emancipation from the rule of custom. For this rule both limits their application and obscures their meaning. Early moral rules are limited in their application. All duties are regarded as duties to the tribe and within the tribe ; and it is only by slow stages that the bonds of tribe and nation have been broken, and that moral ideas have come to be recognised as having universal validity. And the same cause has obscured the meaning of morality. Early morality consists in adherence to custom ; by consequence it concentrates attention upon actions rather than

upon character, upon the external manifestations
of life rather than upon its inward nature. The
emphasis has to be changed—motive and intention,
rather than overt act, have to be accentuated—in
order to bring out the true nature of morality. The
progress of morality thus involves its gradual
emancipation from the external rule of custom and,
at the same time, an increase and deepening of the
reflective factor.

These notes on the history of morality lead up
to our present subject. Morality is internal; it
belongs to the inner life. And this is the mark which
distinguishes it from the law of the land and the
conventions of society. These affect a man from
without, direct or limit his activity, and prescribe
its sphere. Their operation is external; and they
do not touch him at every point : beyond the range
of the actions which they require or forbid there
are wide tracts of conduct to which the laws are
indifferent or which they are unable to cover.
Further, they take account only of things done.
There is an inner circle of personal life which a man
claims as his own, and into which neither positive
law nor social rule is able to penetrate. Morality is
not limited in this way. It rests on a consciousness of the difference between good and evil ; this
consciousness influences the springs of action in a

man's own nature ; it works from within out-
wards, and is capable of affecting every part of his
life.

Law and morality, however, are closely connected.
They were undifferentiated in their origin, and their
subsequent history has been one of constant inter-
action. Moral ideas guide the legislator, and the
moralist has imitated the form and methods of the
jurist. Morality has been often presented as a system
of rules for conduct, or duties : the conception of
moral law has been taken as fundamental. Nor need
objection be taken to this course, provided we bear
in mind that the moral law is not imposed by an
external authority, and does not depend for its
validity on sanctions or penalties. At the same
time, when duty or the moral law is made the
fundamental conception, there is nearly always
a tendency to fix attention primarily on a man's
actions rather than on the man himself, on his
conduct rather than on his character, on what he
does rather than on what he is. Morality is expressed in the imperatives " do this," " abstain from
that " ; and we examine a man's conduct to see
whether the law has been kept. Provided what
is required be performed, and what is forbidden
avoided, we are apt to rest content. Yet it is
possible that the man of exact performance may
remain untouched by the spirit of morality. No

correctness of conduct gives by itself the unity and completeness of the moral life. And this is acknowledged both by the plain man and by the philosopher. Though he have kept all the commandments from his youth up, a man feels that something is still lacking. He asks which is the greatest commandment; he seeks some comprehensive duty which will contain all the others, and in fulfilling which he may have the assurance that he is a good man. The philosopher, also, tries to reduce the varied detail of duty to a single principle, which will express the inward meaning of morality and the ways in which it applies to life.

This unity of principle has been sought in different ways. Sometimes the method has been external, and a general formula has been given for the results which were held to be worthy of attainment; "the greatest happiness of the greatest number" is a formula of this sort. At other times the principle of duty has been found in an attitude of the will itself; and the good will—that is, a will in harmony with the moral law—is said to be the only unqualified good. A view akin to this latter is a consequence of the doctrine that morality is internal. Goodness does not consist in a succession or collection of acts, which we must seek to describe by some general formula. It is a life, which expresses itself in conduct but which has its source in volition. Duty

is the law of the moral life ; but the moral life itself
is realised in character.

A man's character is made both for him and by
him. It is based on his inherited powers and tendencies. It is developed by his experience, including under "experience" both the systematic training which is called education and the countless
influences which the mature as well as the growing
mind receives from physical, social, and mental surroundings. These influences meet with and operate
through an internal factor which modifies the whole
product. This is the individual will. Heredity
provides the basis of character. The environment
gives the external conditions in which it must live
and grow by assimilation of experience and adaptation to the circumstances of life. But the selection
of material and the mode of adaptation depend upon
the nature of the man as a voluntary agent. The man
himself is a factor in producing his own character.
It is through his volition that one action is performed, another left undone ; one career chosen,
another passed by. And these acts and omissions,
in their turn, modify the character of the man to
whom they were due. The disputed question about
free-will need not trouble us here. It is enough
that a man's own volitions are an important factor in
forming his character, and that this voluntary factor
makes praise or blame appropriate in judging him.

No exact measure can be given of the extent to which volition determines character. Some characters seem to be more plastic than others from birth. A trend to virtue or to vice may be born with a man, and in some this trend is more decisive than in others. It is equally clear that circumstances may be favourable or hostile to the development of certain kinds of character. The surroundings into which some men are thrown are of a kind to encourage energy and the orderly rule of the desires and to call forth the higher interests of intellectual, artistic, or social endeavour. Others, again, are so placed that, as we say, circumstances do not give them a chance. No honourable career may be open ; the surroundings may be frankly criminal or wholly frivolous ; and the character tends to be assimilated to the type. These considerations must give us pause should we attempt to assess the merit or guilt of the individual. For such an estimate we should require a full knowledge both of the inherited basis of character and of the social and other conditions under which it took shape. *Tout comprendre c'est tout pardonner*, it has been said. But this epigram too affects omniscience. Those who have known themselves best have not been foremost in asserting that blame is altogether out of place.

The principle is clear enough, though its application is complex and difficult. We do not praise or blame a man for that in his nature with which his will has nothing to do—because he is tall or short, for instance, red-haired or dark. Yet we cannot say that even physical characteristics are altogether outside the range of the moral judgment. The admiration of physical beauty, though frequently conventional and misplaced, has yet within it an element of moral appreciation. A beautiful body suits a beautiful soul and is often its manifestation. The beauty of goodness and the goodness of beauty have even been blended so as to form a single conception ; but this is not the assertion of a fact, but only the expression of a hope that the ideals may not be finally distinct. The connexion between moral and physical excellence is too often broken owing to the intractable material with which the moral will is confronted. In the physical sphere the material is more intractable—more fully determined by conditions independent of volition—than in the case of other aspects of life. But even into it the moral element may enter. It is not by marking off one sphere—for example, what is popularly called conduct—from the other manifestations of life, such as intellectual or even physical characteristics, that we can arrive at a correct account of what belongs to morality. The extent to which volition enters is the only measure of the application of moral predicates. And there is no part of man's nature which lies entirely outside the reach of his will. A man may not be able to add a cubit to his stature, or to remove mountains from his path ; not every man has it in him to be an artist or a mathematician. But he can care for and preserve his bodily health, he can cultivate his intelligence and his artistic sense, and he can strive to climb the mountains that bar his progress.

These considerations enable us to give a meaning to the two terms Natural Virtue and Intellectual Virtue. The terms were used in Greek ethics ; but modern writers find them of doubtful application. The Greek word which we translate " virtue " had not quite the same signification as our term ; to express that meaning fully it had to be qualified by the adjective " moral." The term Natural Virtue (which, however, is of very rare occurrence) was applied to the organic or impulsive basis for virtue in the inherited character—the inborn tendencies which facilitated the growth of specific human excellences. These lie at the foundation of a man's voluntary activities and prepare him beforehand for the cultivation of certain habits of action. In the modern meaning of " virtue," that term cannot be applied to them, because it signifies not merely excellence, but an excellence which arises out of voluntary preferences. It is often difficult, however, to draw the line between qualities which are determined by inherited disposition and qualities which have been acquired by personal and even strenuous volition. What one man attains at the price of a great struggle is entered into by another almost as a birthright. Consequently—apart from any question about individual praise or blame—we are forced to call by the name of virtues all excellences of character which (however they *have been* acquired) *can* be acquired or modified by voluntary effort. So far as any excellence is merely a natural or inherited tendency, it may be the basis of virtue, but is not itself a virtue. But the term virtue is applicable when the quality has become a source of habitual action, provided that it is also capable of being modified by voluntary effort.

Physical capacities are by no means out of all relation to will. By systematic volition a man can greatly modify his original powers in the direction of health and strength ; by idleness or sensual excess he may allow his powers to run to seed and the physiological harmony in which health consists to be disturbed. The strong and healthy man is admired ; the man is blamed who wilfully or negligently ruins his constitution. But we do not put health and bodily strength among the virtues. The reason is twofold : these qualities are only in a small degree amenable to the will, and they cannot be described as habits of willing. Virtue is not only the result of action ; it also tends to action in its turn, whereas these bodily qualities do not originate conduct, though they are amongst its conditions.

The question of the inclusion of intellectual qualities among the virtues must be decided on the same principles, though it involves greater difficulty. All tradition is on the same side, and wisdom has commonly been ranked as the highest of the virtues. But if virtue is a quality of will, a doubt arises. How can we say that wisdom is something in our power, like the other marks of a good character ? We are inclined to look upon it as a gift which we may use or misuse, but which it is not within our power to produce, any more than physical qualities are.

When they described the excellences or virtues of man, both Plato and Aristotle based their classification on the distinction between reason and the non-rational. Plato looked upon the soul as a kind of polity or constitution which consisted of three parts —reason, the spirited or active impulses, and the appetites and desires. Each of these parts had its appropriate function and excellence. The excellence of the first was wisdom, of the second courage, of the third temperance. The notion of excellence or virtue, as used here, was without the special implication of voluntariness which it has in modern usage. It is to Aristotle, however, that the definite distinction of intellectual and moral virtues is due. He defined the former as excellences of the reason, whilst the latter were regarded as excellences due to a proper relation being brought about between reason and desire. There was no hesitation about admitting intellectual qualities as virtues, because the element of volition had not its modern prominence in the conception of virtue. Aristotle himself was the first to make clear the importance of voluntary preference in the formation of virtuous habits. But this analysis was restricted to the case of the moral virtues, and was made to mark a fresh distinction between them and the intellectual virtues : the latter were said to be acquired mainly by instruction, whereas the former were developed by voluntary action out of innate capacity into habits of preference.

If the modern view of virtue, by its emphasis on volition, coincides with what Aristotle called moral virtue, is not the whole intellectual life excluded from its scope ? The inference would be justified only if reason and will were distinct faculties which carried on their business in mutual independence, instead of being, as they are, in intimate connexion. This connexion of reason and will is twofold.

In the first place, intellect or reason is itself voluntary in its exercise. It is not a machine which is simply set in motion by touching the spring of will.

B

It is a mode in which a man acts. In thinking out the solution of a problem, or in forecasting the complicated issues of conduct, a man shows his nature as a voluntary agent as much as in tilling the ground or reaping the harvest, in eating his dinner or fighting his enemy. At least as much voluntary activity is required in following an argument as in transcribing the words in which it is set forth. If a certain aptitude, in the way of intellectual capacity, is required for one process, it is equally true that an aptitude of the nature of physical capacity is required for the other. Either task may be performed with thoroughness, clearness, and impartiality, or in a scrappy, confused, and unfair manner ; and these different kinds of performance arise from and lead to habits which are apt to colour the whole character.

In the second place, as reason is a mode of voluntary activity, so also all action which rises above mere impulse partakes of reason. So clear did this appear to the leading Greek philosophers that they were puzzled to understand how volition could be divorced from reason—how there could be any such thing as unreasonable action. To know what was good seemed to imply willing the good ; for how can a man fail to desire the course which he sees to be best ? From this point of view the virtues were explained as simply different kinds of knowledge : a correct knowledge and estimate of pleasures would be temperance ; a knowledge of what was to be feared and what was not to be feared would be courage ; and so on. This is the Socratic paradox : the will of all men is for the good ; and virtue consists in knowledge. The view is obviously at variance with the facts ; yet it would seem to be no further from the truth of things than the contrary view, often put forward in modern times, that reason can never be a motive to the will. This latter view is as great a paradox as the characteristic doctrine of Socrates, although it may be stated so as to appear almost a truism. If reason is regarded as a distinct faculty in man, then it may be thought that its quasi-mechanical operations go on in a sphere of their own, and that it is only when they terminate in some pleasant idea that volition is set in motion. But reason is not restricted to the manipulation of abstract terms and relations. Such abstract reasoning may very well have only an indirect bearing or no bearing at all upon action. The solution of the famous question, How many angels can dance on the point of a needle ? will sew on no buttons. But reason is concerned primarily with concrete interests ; these interests stimulate and sustain the reasoning process, and tend to enforce its conclusion. The real difficulty, therefore, is not to see how it is possible for reason to influence volition, but to understand its frequent failure to do so. The difficulty is explained by the want of perfect harmony which exists between the constituent parts of man's nature. Desire is in origin allied to impulse ; and impulse has its roots in deep-seated hereditary tendencies which have nothing to do with reason. It is therefore easy for conflict to arise between desire and reason. But these cases of disharmony always tend to equilibrium. Either the desires are brought into subjection to reason, or else the repeated victories of desire result in obscuring and perverting the decisions of the intellect until immoral conduct comes to be supported by immoral principles.

The term intellectual virtue, therefore, is not a misnomer, although it does not, as with Aristotle, indicate a class distinct from moral virtue. There are certain excellences which belong to a man in his capacity as a thinking being, and these may be called intellectual virtues. Further, there is an element of thought in all action ; and, unless a man's conduct is to some extent enlightened by a view of its end, we hardly speak of it as virtuous : his temperance will be regarded as only the result of a happy moderation in the strength of his passions. his courage as only an insensibility to fear, and so on. In true temperance the impulses are controlled by the conception of an end worthy of a man's desire ; in true courage it is in pursuit of a high purpose that pain and danger are readily faced. The purpose or end, which, in this way, is involved in all virtuous character, cannot be formed without reason. Virtue—if we take the term to include all the characteristics which we call virtuous—is nothing less than the realisation of goodness in human character ; and it implies some idea—though not necessarily a complete, or even a clear, idea—of the good to be realised. This is the element of truth in the Socratic paradox that virtue is knowledge.

An account of the moral life, from the point of view of moral worth, must take the form of a description and analysis of the virtues, that is, of the qualities which the moral consciousness of men regards as exhibiting goodness in human character. This realisation of goodness in man presents a two-sided development, an individual or personal and a social. From the individual point of view we have to look to the way in which a man's capacities are brought into rational order and system. But the development of individual character does not proceed by itself. Its nature and value can be understood only by taking into account the social relations and institutions into which the individual was born and which he in his turn helps to build up or modify.

These two aspects are inseparable in the moralisation of man. The moral ideal has to enter into his

own personal nature, so that impulse and desire
are made to work in harmony with reason and the
highest possible perfection is given to the development of his powers. This is the personal aspect of
virtue ; and, as the greatest obstacle in its way is the
power of unreasoning impulse and sensuous desire,
we may say that personal virtue has to do in the
first place with the suppression of sensualism. But
this suppression of sensualism is accomplished in
the virtuous character side by side with the suppression of selfishness. Man is a member of society
—of the commonwealth of man—and the realisation of his own nature must be carried out in connexion with a world of related persons, who in
virtue of their personality have equal claims to
moral development. This negative element—or
element of suppression—involved in the moral life
does not require the extinction either of one's own
personality in presence of others, or of desire and the
pleasures of satisfaction in presence of reason. It is
the moralisation not the annihilation of ambition
and desire that is demanded, the finding of one's
true self in others' good as well as one's own, and the
bringing of one's sensuous nature into harmony with
the realisation of a rational personality.

If we make this fundamental distinction of
Personal and Social the basis of a classification of
the virtues, we must bear in mind the limits of the

distinction. The individual self and the community
are not centres of different circles ; they may rather
be said to be the two foci in relation to which we
may describe the course of human activities. If we
follow only a part of the course of these activities,
it may appear as if our actions were determined by
their relation to one point only ; followed out, all
our actions are seen to stand in relation to both
points. No virtues are purely personal ; no vices
can be indulged without detriment to society,
though their most obvious effect may be on the
individual. Temperance and intemperance, courage
and cowardice entail manifold consequences to
society ; wisdom is the true pilot of the state, which
is wrecked if folly be at the helm. The social
virtues, again—justice, benevolence, and the like—
are in their essence personal qualities : but, in their
case, not only the conditions which call them forth,
but their whole scope and character are due to
society. We may therefore define Personal Virtues
as those excellences of character which exhibit the
due ordering and regulation of the lower by the
higher nature, and the culture or development of
this harmonious personality. Social Virtues, on
the other hand, are those excellences of personal
character which exhibit the individual in harmonious
relation with other persons—respecting their rights
and promoting the common welfare. And the two

classes are interdependent : without the personal virtues social good is not likely to be rightly striven after ; without the social virtues, the personal character is a monstrosity—seeking individual good in isolation from the community to which all qualities are due and in which all good must be realised.

Further, there are in human life dispositions and activities connected with our attitude not merely to personal and social ends, but to human life as a whole and its final meaning. These are apt to elude exact definition ; for the object which determines their scope is not one object amongst others presented in experience. Yet it is this attitude which gives completeness to human character ; and room must be found, under a third division, for virtues corresponding to what have been called Theological Virtues.

CLASSIFICATION OF THE CARDINAL VIRTUES

I. Personal virtues, or excellences not de-
    pendent for their meaning on social
    relations :—
        (1) exhibiting self-control,
            (*a*) the control of pleasures   = TEMPERANCE.
            (*b*) the control of pains and
                direction of conduct in
                spite of pain,   } = COURAGE.
              involving thus
        (2) self-culture,
            exhibited especially in the
              organisation and direction of } = WISDOM.
              conduct by reason

II. Social virtues, or excellences arising out of
       social relations :—
        (1) due regard for the rights of others = JUSTICE.
        (2) due regard for the needs of others = BENEVOLENCE

III. Religious virtues, or excellences in the
       personal attitude to the ultimate meaning
       of life.

CHAPTER II

THE virtues of personal life are to be regarded both
from the side of control and from the side of culture.
On the one hand the varied impulses and desires
have to be regulated so as not to interfere with the
realisation of the moral ideal. Man must be master
of himself, neither swayed hither and thither by each
desire as it arises, nor under the influence of some
master passion which has obtained power in spite of
the moral reason. This element of self-control is
included in the full meaning of self-culture. But
self-culture means much more. It is pre-eminently
a positive and active attitude, as self-control is an
attitude of restraint. Self-culture means such a
development of personal capacities as leads to the
realisation of the greatest possible perfection of one's
nature. It is the active side of personal virtue, as
self-control is its passive side.

Within this distinction we may find place for three
out of the four Cardinal Virtues, which, since the
time of Plato, have been held to express the leading
characteristics of all that is admirable in the moral
life. The moral consciousness of Christian as well as

non-Christian times has accepted this account of the qualities on which virtuous habits " hinge," and it is therefore well to retain, as far as possible, the old terminology and divisions. Justice, of course, belongs to the field of social morality ; but temperance, courage, and wisdom may be taken as leading personal virtues. Temperance and courage might be said to signify the due regulation of the inferior elements in man's nature and thus to be branches of self-control, while wisdom expresses the positive perfection of that which is highest in man, and is thus the most striking and brilliant quality in what is called self-culture.

But this statement does less than justice to the nature of courage. All that we mean by temperance is expressed by the term self-control ; but the same term does not express the full meaning of courage. It is true that, for courage as for temperance, the impulses need to be held in restraint. Further, it is true that a close parallel may be drawn between the restraint exercised in temperance and that required for courage. But the latter has a positive and active quality which does not belong to the former. As temperance may be said to consist in due restraint of the tendencies to pleasure, so in courage the fear of pain is controlled, and man is armed against the obstacles in his path. In Plato's account of them, both temperance and courage

might be regarded as different kinds of self-control :
temperance being the due regulation of the desires
and appetites, while courage is the rational guidance
of the spirited or combative part of the soul—a part
which has, however, as he asserts, a natural affinity
with reason and tendency to side with it against
the usurpation of desire. This distinction is of
decisive importance. In the cultivation of temperance the desires require to be *restrained* by reason,
whereas it is *guidance* by reason that is chiefly needed
to produce courage. Only a partial view of courage
can be got by regarding it as a case of self-control.
This is its passive side. In its positive nature it
tends to manifest itself as the type of active virtue,
which pursues its path undeterred by pain and
difficulty and danger.

The fundamental element in human activity is of
the nature of impulse. The impulses, as they arise
and lead on to action, are not altogether without
order or system : they occur in response to some
definite kind of stimulus. Nor are they entirely
blind : they may show adaptation to an end even
when the agent has no conscious purpose before
himself. When a definite impulse, with its special
emotional tone, follows upon its appropriate stimulus,
and when the response is adapted to some vital need,
we have the characteristic features of instinct. The

instinct, with its system and purposiveness, is part of the mental and physical endowment of the individual as that has been determined for him by heredity. In the life of instinct he enters into and assimilates the experience of the race—but without deliberation or foresight. With the growth of mind, a man begins to form conscious purposes and to reflect upon the best means for realising them. The processes of the instinctive life are supplemented, and to some extent displaced, by an order governed by reflection ; ends are sought which instinct did not provide, and they are sought by means which it did not devise ; volition and intelligence take the place of automatism ; the moral life becomes possible.

But the life of conscious purpose has always as its basis the material of impulse. The appetites, which aim at supplying the needs of the physical organism, give rise to the most persistent and, nearly always, the strongest impulses. But other objects, as they excite interest and pleasure accompanies their presence, occasion similar impulses and originate definite desires. The relative strength of these impulses varies greatly from the outset in different constitutions ; they appear in an unsystematic way ; and order is introduced among them gradually by reflection on their ends or results, and by means of the education which anticipates and guides such reflection.

In Plato's *Republic*, in which the soul of man is compared to a civic community, the desires are made to represent the industrial portion of the population ; and, as the sole duty of the working-class in Plato's state is to do their work in obedience to the laws of the guardians or rulers, so and in the same way the function of desire in the soul consists simply in obedience to the rule of reason. The analogy, of course, is not to a democratic state in which the people rule : that would suggest to Plato the mob-rule of desires in a man, and would, in his view, be little better than the tyranny of some master passion to which it would infallibly tend. His ideal state is an aristocracy in which the people do not rule but only obey. When the same doctrine is extended to the soul, it would seem to lead to a view of the desires as without value of their own, and thus to an ascetic interpretation of the virtue of temperance.

Yet the peculiarly Greek virtue of moderation suggests the orderly rule rather than the conquest and extermination of desire. The word which we translate temperance is, says Jowett, " a peculiarly Greek notion which may also be rendered moderation, modesty, discretion, wisdom, without completely exhausting by all these terms the various associations of the word. It may be described as *mens sana in corpore sano*, the harmony or due proportion of the higher and lower elements of human nature, which 'makes a man his own master,' according to the definition of the *Republic*."

The doctrine that temperance consists in moderate use is most fully worked out by Aristotle, although he has a somewhat narrow view of its application, for he limits his consideration of it to certain bodily desires or appetites. A habit of enjoying these in moderation is the excellence in which, as he holds, temperance consists, while asceticism or abstinence would seem to be as much a vice as excess. In this view of temperance we have perhaps the best example of Aristotle's characteristic doctrine of the " mean "—a doctrine which he uses to fix the exact measure of each of the moral virtues. In all the moral virtues we have reason applied to a certain content of impulse or desire ; and the doctrine of the mean is an attempt to give a precise account of the measure of this application—an account which is at the same time an explicit working out of the doctrine of moderation traditional in Greek ethics from the time of the Seven Sages. The doctrine, however, is not so precise as it looks. Aristotle is careful to point out that his " mean state " is not an absolute or arithmetical mean. He guards himself beforehand from the reproach brought against him long afterwards by Kant, that he made merely a quantitative difference between virtue and vice. The mean or moderate state in which virtue consists is relative to the matter with which it deals, and is determined by the judgment of the man of moral insight. The weight of the whole Aristotelian doctrine of virtue thus rests upon the judgment of the good man or man of moral insight. The precision of the doctrine of the mean is really lost in the explanation that only a relative mean is intended. All that remains of it is that every virtuous habit lies between two opposed extremes. At what distance it stands from each cannot be told until the opinion of the morally good man has been taken. Thus, no measure is given of the amount of use which is consistent with moderation, although the point is plainly made that temperance implies use, not abstinence.

But the question may be asked, Is the rule of temperance due and moderate use, as Aristotle held, or the complete suppression of desire as the ascetics of all ages have maintained? Put in this form the question admits of but one answer, and yet that answer is hardly satisfactory. Asceticism is the gospel of pessimism. Only if the natural impulses and desires of men are wholly evil can virtue consist in their suppression. Now these impulses and desires form the material basis of human life. Even speculative contemplation could not survive their complete extinction. The most logical pessimism, accordingly, is that which identifies the suppression of desire with the extinction of life.

The ascetic view denies the possibility of moralising ordinary life : the desires, impulses, and appetites of man. It is content only with their complete suppression : even although its end may be the monkish ideal of a future life of bliss to be obtained by the mortification of the flesh. This view has never been so popular as to endanger the continuance of human or social life. It affects only the anæmic persons in whom passion is a negligible quantity, or else the comparatively small number of people who, with strong passions, have also a resolute power of self-mastery. Yet these latter are often among the best of their race ; and it makes them desert the real battlefield of human morality, to seek victory on a field with which the race has little concern, since victory there can only be reached through death.

The more immediate danger of the ascetic view of life is that it sets up—as was done in the times of monasticism, and as is still sometimes done to-day— a dual standard of virtue : a " higher life," which abstains from marriage, from the eating of flesh and the drinking of wine, even from social intercourse with fellow-men, and from the ordinary decencies of life ; and a lower standard, which permits such things to the weaker wills of ordinary men.

c

But it would be unfair to include in this condemnation every demand for abstinence. A true ethical spirit is often to be seen in such a demand. It may be required by the conditions of the personal life, or may be due to its social surroundings. The measure of temperance cannot be expressed by the simple rule " be moderate " any more than by the simple rule " abstain." The former may be nearer the true reading of virtuous performance : but its vagueness needs elucidation by a nearer view of its meaning, and this nearer view may give a partial or occasional justification to abstinence.

In all cases, we have to ask what the motive or purpose is of the self-control in which temperance consists. Is it not the highest possible development of our nature both for personal and for social ends ? And, from the personal as well as from the social point of view, the rule of moderation in desire may not always exclude abstinence. Two elements are involved in the temperate life. The first is self-mastery : the passions must be so under control, that a man may know and feel himself their master and not liable to be turned aside by them from achieving the end of his moral endeavour. The second is regulation : the bringing of impulse and desire into such order that, instead of opposing, they may subserve a moral purpose. The function of the appetites in all animal life shows how they may

serve important ends. Thus the primary appetites
lead to the preservation of the individual and the
race, and in man they become the bonds of friendship
and family affection. In this way the merely
natural impulse is moralised by being made the
guardian, not of life alone but also, in a measure, of
the higher life.

But circumstances, or the inherited disposition of
the individual, may give any one impulse a strength
far greater than is salutary in the interests of the
moral and social life. This superabundant strength
is most clearly characteristic of the primary appetites.
They have to secure the preservation of the individual
life and the perpetuation of the human race, and their
importance, accordingly, is so great—especially in
the pre-reflective stages of human development—
that we find them now clamant and powerful to a
degree which often appals the reason. Hence it is
that for the due regulation of desire, mastery of
desire may be regarded as an essential condition.
The governing element in the polity of man's life
has to be trained to rule, and the subject desires have
to be habituated to obedience. It may be sometimes
necessary in the interests of the moral life to abstain
altogether from indulging a desire, lest it grow by
what it feeds on until it obtain such power as to be
an obstacle to the performance of important service.
This is perhaps not seldom the case in desires which

are due to social convention or to the special qualities
of some natural object, though they may not have
any immediate bearing upon morality. Thus it is
told of a late distinguished man of affairs, that " he
once smoked a cigar and found it so delicious that he
never smoked again." The need of self-control will
arise sometime, and that man alone is prepared for
emergencies who has practised the art of self-sacrifice
and trained his reason to bear rule in the soul. The
late William James—who was never afraid to point
a moral—has gone so far as to lay down the practical
maxim : " *Keep the faculty of effort alive in you by
a little gratuitous exercise every day.* That is, be
systematically ascetic or heroic in little unnecessary
points, do every day or two something for no other
reason than that you would rather not do it, so that
when the hour of dire need draws nigh, it may find
you not unnerved and untrained to stand the test.
Asceticism of this sort is like the insurance which a
man pays on his house and goods. The tax does him
no good at the time and may possibly never bring
him a return. But if the fire *does* come, his having
paid it will be his salvation from ruin. So with the
man who has daily inured himself to habits of con-
centrated attention, energetic volition, and self-
denial in unnecessary things. He will stand like
a tower when everything rocks around him, and when
his weaker fellow-mortals are winnowed like chaff

in the blast." Perhaps most men are so placed that they do not need deliberately to seek these occasions for self-denial. But whether they are sought out—as James recommends—or whether they come unsought, they are essential to the training of character.

When we take into account the social aspect of the virtue of temperance, there may appear to be still further room for abstinence. When a man drinks no wine for fear he may become a drunkard, we commend his conduct, but think his self-control short of the highest. He is able to subdue desire, but not to regulate it. But when he drinks no wine lest others may become drunkards, we do not thus qualify our admiration. The need for such self-sacrifice arises from the fact that personal and social development do not keep step in their progress. The same community contains individuals at all stages of moral and intellectual development : men of strength of will and high purpose on the one hand, and on the other men who need every adventitious aid to strengthen their weak germ of self-control, and who are unable to understand any rule of the desires which allows them to play any part at all in life. For the sake of such, and at the call of social duty, the higher culture which uses without abusing may bend itself to non-usage, and neither drink wine nor eat meat lest a brother offend. Abstinence of this kind, however, would seem to be limited in its scope, because the grounds for it are occasional and temporary. It is when the desires have no essential connexion with what is good and admirable in life, that there may be a call to forgo their enjoyment altogether lest others fall into excess ; and, as self-control is more widely spread throughout the community, the need for such abstinence for the sake of example will disappear.

A zeal against fleshly lust has led almost every moral and religious teacher to lay his ban upon some natural desire or other in the interests of the moral progress of the community he was addressing. The flesh has been contrasted with the spirit as the source of all evil ; and a pattern of holiness exhibited in a purely spiritual or purely intellectual life. But such life is not the life of man. His highest attainable life does not abolish the life of sense, but purifies and ennobles it, by bringing it into harmony with a high purpose and by gathering its forces together to fulfil a worthy end. It is in this way that not the body only, but the whole framework of life, may be fitted to become, in religious language, a " temple of the Holy Ghost."

The leading characteristic of the intemperate life is a negative one. It is without order or system. The intemperate man is swayed by each impulse as it arises and asserts its strength. He never

achieves a stable character, or, if he does, it is only
through the overmastering force of a single impulse
to which repeated indulgence has given the lead in
his life.   It has been urged that a strong impulse of
this kind can only be overcome by finding a stronger
impulse which is able to wrest from it its place.
Emphasis used to be laid on the moral importance of
this view by Dr Chalmers in expounding a favourite
doctrine of his—" the expulsive power of a new
affection."   And there is a certain amount of truth
in the doctrine.   A strong impulse cannot be overcome by an intellectual notion.   The merely formal
conviction that the impulse is bad, is not enough to
reduce its strength.   The evil affection must be
replaced by good affections.   Yet the view is only
partially correct ; it does not recognise the organic
unity of mental facts—even such different facts as
desire and understanding.   The moral life is not
like some ancient battlefield in which the issue is
determined by single combat between two champions.
The metaphor of the battlefield may not be in-
applicable to many of its incidents, but even then it
is opposing forces, not single champions, that are
matched against one another.   The moral life is an
organised system, and its progress is a process of
growth, in which material is both assimilated and
rejected.

The material is impulse which finds its term in the

enjoyment of an object. The earliest moral training consists in the application of measure or moderation to the gratification of these impulses. This involves the restraint of impulse—a restraint which is seen to be adapted to the realisation of a desire, and involves more or less complicated adjustments of acts to ends. In this way impulses and desires become co-ordinated with reference to their purpose. The merely natural impulses are thus brought into complex mutual relations which receive form and unity from some rational idea. The highest conception we can form of a moralised life is one in which complete unity of character and purpose has been achieved by the harmonious subjection of all impulses and systems of impulses to the idea of the Good. This is the ideal of the temperate man, and, in its completeness, it is also the ideal of the perfectly virtuous man : for only in subordination to the highest moral ideal can complete co-ordination and regulation of impulses be established. Even if this unity were realised, human character would still be a very complex system—consisting not merely in the ordering of particular impulses, but in the unification of many such orders or subordinate systems corresponding to the various classes of needs and desires which enter into life. Our material needs, our family relationships, our friendships, our businesses, our favourite pursuits, all form such minor volitional systems, or, as they have been called, "universes of desire." It is a mark of an imperfect character when these various groups of desire and interest are not co-ordinated—do not together make up a system : so that a man's life is torn and disconnected, and no common thread of purpose runs through it. And it is a mark of a bad character when a volitional system which is only fitted to fill a subordinate place in life is allowed to dominate the whole, when sense or self is the centre upon which a man's whole world of desire turns. Again, the training of character takes place not wholly or chiefly by exciting new interests, but by introducing order into the grouping of interests, so that the different universes of desire may be systematised in a harmonious life.

Now the ordinary view of temperance is that it implies the preservation of at least so much order in one's volitional systems that a man is the slave neither of each impulse as it arises, nor of that system of impulses whose end is sensuous gratification. But the principle admits of extension. If we extend the use of the term temperance so as to include not merely the control of sensuous desire, but the control of all desires which obstruct the highest moral performance in our power, the principle and root-idea of the ancient virtue of temperance are still preserved, while it has a fresh applica-

tion given to it.   Universes of desire which are far
removed from the vulgar temptations of sense,
and are in themselves of high moral worth, yet, for
men with certain gifts and in certain surroundings,
may not give promise of the noblest performance
in their power.   A man is said to " deny himself "
who postpones one volitional system, or universe of
desire, to another which has greater moral claims
upon him : who gives of his substance that others
may not want, who toils at his business to give his
children a good start in the world, who lives laborious
days in the service of science or of art, or in hope that
he may leave a name which the world will not
willingly let die.   For these interests and such as
these, he restrains a whole class of clamorous
desires and turns his back on what the world calls
pleasure.

But still higher ends than fortune or fame may call
him ; and the question may arise in his life whether
he is to cultivate the universe of desires connected
with his intellectual interests and artistic ideals,
or whether even these must be postponed to realising
for others than himself the conditions of a worthy
human life.   No simple answer can be given to the
question.   It is not possible to lay down any definite
rule for deciding between the rival claims of such
different circles of interest as those of higher personal
culture and social benevolence.   Much must depend

on each man's special gifts and on the special circumstances in which he is placed. Yet moral judgment is not silent on the point. We do not hesitate to condemn as selfish the man who ignores the claims of human brotherhood, even although he may be on the trail of an unclassified worm or be compiling a " key to all the mythologies." And we feel that the man who has the instincts and powers of the artist, philosopher, or discoverer, and yet has proved himself able to subordinate these noble desires in the service of other men less fortunately placed than himself, has shown the noblest form of self-sacrifice— a self-sacrifice which expresses the highest development of the virtue of temperance.

" There are men, we know," says T. H. Green, who has insisted on this point, " who with the keenest sensibility to such pleasures as those of ' gratified ambition and love of learning,' yet deliberately forgo them; who shut themselves out from an abundance of æsthetic enjoyments which would be open to them, as well as from those of family life ; and who do this in order to meet the claims which the work of realising the possibilities of the human soul in society—a work a hundredfold more complex as it presents itself to us than as it presented itself to Aristotle—seems to make upon them. Such sacrifices are made now, as they were not made in the days of the Greek philosophers, and in that sense a higher type of living is known among us ; not because there are men now more ready to fulfil recognised duties than there were then, but because with the altered structure of society men have become alive to claims to which, with the most open eye and heart, they could not be alive then." Such sacrifices, we may add, exhibit the greatest trial and greatest triumph of modern cultured goodness—the triumph of the ideal of human brotherhood over the selfish development even of the highest part of the individual nature.

The full and final universe of desire must be one in which the narrowness of individual ambition and individual culture, as well as the grossness of sensual appetite, has been overcome. Sense must be permeated by reason, and reason itself inspired by the ideal of a common humanity. Among the circles or systems of personal interest, the social self asserts its claim as pre-eminently the moral self. A society of intemperate men, in the narrower sense of the term, that is, of men ruled only by sensuous desire, has in itself the seeds of disintegration and decay. The citizens must discipline their own members that they may be fitted both to submit to and to exercise the control and ordered activity that constitute a commonwealth. And social progress requires a corresponding development in this power of personal control—the regulation not merely of what is called the " lower nature," but of all lesser interests, in presence of the spirit of social unity—the recognition of the claims of mankind upon the devotion of men.

CHAPTER III

It is not without reason that courage holds the fore most place in Aristotle's list of the virtues. Plato's order was different : temperance coming first as the control of appetite and desire, and next to it courage as the due regulation of certain higher impulses, combative or spirited, which act as watch-dogs of the soul and protect it from danger. This view better reveals the essential nature because the true purpose of courage. It is the type of active virtue which triumphs over difficulties and dangers for the sake of a worthy end.

But courage, in its beginnings, is something less dignified. It is not so much the guidance of the active impulses which guard the soul against evil and, as Plato has it, naturally side with reason against desire. It has to perform another and inferior office : to act as a restraint on what is base rather than as the guide of higher powers. It has to control the ignoble impulse under which a man tends to turn his back to the foe, to flee from danger, to tremble at the shock of fear, to be unmanned by a touch of pain. Hence courage may be said to be

the first element, the basis of manliness ; it would
seem to be the primary excellence which appears in
the triumph of the moral over the natural man.

The control of fear—of certain kinds of fear, at
any rate—seems to arise earlier in the history of
races than the control of the appetites whose satisfaction brings sensual pleasure. It is the strength
of these impulses that often impels men and animals
to put aside fear and face danger in pursuit of food
or mates. Mastery of pain, in this sense, precedes
mastery of pleasure. The virtue which first raises
man to organised civic existence is the virtue of
courage. The very existence of a young community
commonly rests on the fighting quality of its members;
and the courage required is courage in presence of
the dangers of war and battle. This is the primitive
type of manliness ; and to this quality the warlike
Romans gave the characteristic name of *virtus* :
the man's excellence rather than the woman's, for
the woman kept the home while he defended it with
his sword from hostile attack.

This is the primitive virtue ; and we are often
reminded, from unexpected quarters, of the prominent place it occupies even in the modern conscience. " Every man," said Dr Johnson, " thinks
meanly of himself for not having been a soldier, or
not having been at sea. . . . Were Socrates and
Charles the Twelfth of Sweden both present in any

company, and Socrates to say, ' Follow me and hear
a lecture in philosophy ' ;   and Charles, laying his
hand on his sword, to say, ' Follow me and dethrone
the Czar,' a man would be ashamed to follow
Socrates.   Sir, the impression is universal. . . . The
profession of soldiers and sailors has the dignity of
danger.   Mankind reverence those who have got
over fear, which is so general a weakness."

Courage has been often represented as rather a
physical quality than a moral virtue.   But the
difference, in this respect, between it and the other
virtues is only a difference of degree.   All the virtues
are connected with organic conditions ; they are all
built upon impulsive or instinctive tendencies.   In
courage, the impulsive basis is more obvious than
it is in the case of the other virtues.   The ability to
look danger calmly in the face, and to bear pain
with unblenched cheek, is certainly very largely a
matter of inherited constitution ; and it is perhaps
on this account that we find Plato sometimes
drawing a broad line of distinction between courage
and the other virtues.   " Do you ask me," he says,
" what is that one thing which I call virtue and then
again speak of as two, one part being courage, and
the other wisdom ?   I will tell you how that occurs :
one of them has to do with fear ; in this the beasts
also participate, and quite young children—I mean
courage ; for a courageous temper is a gift of nature,

and not of reason. But without reason there never has been, nor is, nor will be a wise and understanding soul."

Courage, however, is like the other virtues in that it admits of training. The power to stand up against fear is not altogether out of our control ; the constitutional basis of courage, like the constitutional basis of temperance, may be developed, or may be allowed to degenerate, by the kind of voluntary activity carried out, until courage or cowardice becomes habitual. It is true that, in the case of courage, more depends upon inherited constitution, less is in the power of the will, than in the case of temperance. But in neither case is either constitutional tendency or volitional power all-sufficient ; and courage admits of being strengthened and directed by means fundamentally the same as those which are employed for education in temperance.

The view of courage taken by Aristotle is in its extent much more restricted than would be required to suit all the demands of modern life. He practically limits it to the quality first produced by the necessities of civic life and most essential in the citizen-soldier : the control of fear in presence of the dangers of war and battle, for these are the most terrible of dangers, involving death. That man, he says, is in the strict sense courageous " who

D

fearlessly faces an honourable death, and all sudden emergencies which involve death."

Even here, dealing simply with the brave man's attitude to the dangers of battle, we may distinguish two very different kinds or forms of courage. There is, in the first place, the kind of courage which enables a man to meet a sudden emergency—to attack or defend, without reflection or deliberation, when time for these may fail. For this the habit ingrained in the inherited constitution is most effective. It is, we may say, a quality of the blood— which fires at a sudden shock, and is fired to fight and not to flee. And this kind of courage—being immediate and almost instinctive in its operation— is most difficult to produce by practice.

In the second place, there is the courage which is a habit of deliberate choice, by which a man is able calmly to select and follow the path strewn with dangers if it be the path of honour. It is this latter kind of courage that may be said to be most clearly a moral virtue, because it is a product and characteristic of the reflective will. The impetuous courage of uncivilised races is most commonly of the former kind—fierce and relentless in the onset, but unable to stand and continue the fight when once the charge has been withstood and the line broken, and thus, in warfare, usually unfit to cope with the disciplined courage of civilised armies.

The contrast between these two kinds of courage may be illustrated by a scene described by R. L. Stevenson in his novel *Catriona*. Alan Breck and David Balfour are on the sands of Gullane watching for the boat which is to carry one of them to France and safety, while behind the sandhills, half a mile away, the soldiers of the Lord Advocate are hastening to anticipate the boat's crew. It is a race for life in which the men whose lives are at stake can neither further nor hinder the issue. And the two men take the experience differently. Alan Breck, the " bonny fighter," and hero of the famous battle of the Round House, who has faced sudden death a hundred times and never flinched, is now almost unmanned, runs forward a few paces and then back, enters the water and again retreats, while his younger companion doggedly awaits the issue. " For auld, cauld, dour, deidly courage," says Alan to him, " I am not fit to hold a candle to yourself." This is the courage not of hot blood, but of strong will and steady principle, and much more than the other realises what is required of courage as a moral virtue—that it be a control of fear with a noble or worthy purpose in view. If we may trust that veracious historian M. Alexandre Dumas the elder, this was the kind of courage which distinguished the Protestant leader King Henry of Navarre. His cheek blenched and limbs trembled at the opening of a battle ; he was constitutionally a coward ; but he led in the thickest of the fight : for he was brave of deliberate purpose, for the sake of honour and glory.

This distinction between the courage of physical constitution and the courage of deliberate purpose, which is a moral virtue, must be supplemented by another distinction, which has been already foreshadowed by the view that has been taken of courage as involving elements both of self-control and of self-culture. The passive courage which can endure all things is not always accompanied by the active spirit which prompts to great enterprise in spite of difficulty and danger. Endurance is the passive side of the virtue of courage ; and, in times of oppression and persecution, there may be little scope for any other form of courage. It may even be that, to some types of character, and at certain periods, no opportunity has been offered—or has been apparent—for infusing one's ideals into the actual circumstances of life : to bear manfully the evil of the world has seemed to be its only good. This was the dominant note of the Christian ideal of courage as described both by early and by medieval writers. To the things of the present world it presented a mainly negative attitude. Cicero's term *fortitudo* for the cardinal virtue of courage, adopted by St Ambrose, and passing from him to the medieval moralists, came in this way to have with them the prevailing signification of endurance. Forgiveness in return for injury, meekness in presence of the proud claims of others, were essentially connected with the new Christian idea of the brotherhood of man. But they were also allied to that meaner view of the value of all temporal concerns, which the assurance of man's spiritual dignity and destiny implied, or seemed to imply. Only when a prospect seemed to arise of remoulding the temporal order by the spiritual factor, and rebuilding a " city of God " upon earth, was it possible for Christian courage to resume the active characteristics of energy and enterprise which marked the old Pagan virtue, and to carry them forward to wider issues.

The undue emphasis often laid on the physical basis of courage has obscured its connexion with the virtuous life as a whole. But we look upon it wrongly when we regard it as a solitary virtue which can easily coexist with all sorts of vice. No more than the other virtues is courage able to stand alone and to stand firm. It is true that warfare is commonly signalised by wild outbursts of the natural passions, when the goods and persons of the vanquished lie at the mercy of the victors. But the outburst is in part due to the enforced restraint of the days of preparation for the conflict. Especially as warfare and warlike training are developed, the connexion

of courage with other virtues of character becomes
apparent. Thus, the education of the Spartan
youth was a training in temperance—that is, in pro-
longed abstinence from many natural pleasures—
at the same time that it was pre-eminently a training
in the control of that fear of pain and danger which
stands in the way of the survival of a people sur-
rounded by enemies.

As in the case of temperance, so in that of courage,
the purity of the ancient notion, as set forth by
Aristotle, admits of defence. Its source is internal :
its spring is the good will which is dominated by a
purpose held to be worth the effort. But the virtue
is applied by him to a narrow field. The State, with
its need for defence, is the source of the honourable
or noble end for the sake of which the brave man acts
bravely. It is characteristic of Aristotle that, in the
last resort, the State—the social order and social
opinion—determines the extent of all the moral
virtues, except, indeed, of that pure life of contemplation to which the State itself is subservient.
And the same conception dominates Plato's thought,
though he has allowed himself greater freedom with
actual conditions in his construction of the ideal
State within which virtue operates. "There are
two things," he says, "which give victory—confidence before enemies and fear of disgrace before
friends. . . . There are two things which should be

cultivated in the soul ; first, the greatest courage ;
secondly, the greatest fear." Yet Greek ethics was
not without a wider notion. Socrates had indicated
the validity of a higher law than that of the State ;
and Cynics and Stoics, often with a harshness which
betokens the struggling of a new idea imperfectly
apprehended, had emphasised their readiness to
overcome the "fear of disgrace before friends"
in carrying out their ideal of the wise or good man's
life.

This is the root-element in what is called moral
courage. The limitation of the name is unjustifiable :
for the control of the fear of physical evil may exhibit
a moral virtue of character quite as much as the
control of the fear of social evil—of disgrace or
ridicule amongst those who determine the opinion
of the community—in which so-called moral courage
consists. Yet the term, although unnecessarily
qualified, indicates a widening of our moral conceptions. Not to fear ridicule or social contumely
in pursuit of a good object is as true a form of
courage as not to fear shot or shell in defence of one's
country. In both the high purpose controls the fear
of evil—whether the evil be to limb and life, or to
social repute. And to brave the latter loss shows
that our moral ideal is more securely rooted than in
social institutions or opinion.

In one stage of social development, the enthusiasts

who desire to bring about fundamental changes of life and thought are tortured and put to death. A more refined civilisation laughs them to scorn. And so the robust Dr Johnson regarded persecution as a test of truth : are men willing to die for their creed ? The politer Earl of Shaftesbury looked to ridicule as the specific against superstition : the errors of enthusiasm are to be laughed down by the raillery of the educated. The criteria are different ; but the moral attitude is the same which enables the brave man to follow without fear what he regards as noble or true, whether the pains that threaten him be those of physical torment or of social scorn. What we call moral courage is therefore not a new and purer form of the virtue ; it is only a fresh application of it, which involves willingness to endure social as well as physical penalties.

Although Aristotle was thinking mainly of the dangers of battle, he means by courage a state of heart and will, and not merely physical prowess ; and he accordingly distinguishes true courage from various false or spurious kinds of courage. Using slightly different names from his, we may enumerate these spurious—perhaps they should rather be called imperfect—kinds of courage as the courage of hope, which seeks only reward or distinction ; the courage of fear, which is simply to avoid disgrace or punishment ; the courage of experience, as that of regular troops matched against irregulars ; the courage of rage, which is merely an animal quality and lacks reflection ; the courage of the sanguine man, who overestimates his chances ; and the courage of ignorance, where the danger is unknown. And to these we might add the courage of insensibility, where neither the worth of life nor the pain of death and wounds touches the imagination : a courage due to sluggish emotions rather than to the deliberate choice of the good ; and the courage of despair, in which life itself is no longer valued : whereas the highest courage, as Aristotle himself remarks, is manifested where a happy life is risked or relinquished for a noble end.

The brave man, therefore, is simply the moral man in presence of danger and triumphing over fear :

> " But who, if he be called upon to face
> Some awful moment to which heaven has joined
> Great issues, good or bad for human kind,
> Is happy as a Lover ; and attired
> With sudden brightness like a man inspired
> And, through the heat of conflict, keeps the law
> In calmness made, and sees what he foresaw.
>
> .   .   .   .   .   .
>
> Who, whether praise of him must walk the earth
> For ever, and to noble deeds give birth,
> Or he must fall, to sleep without his fame,
> And leave a dead unprofitable name—
> Finds comfort in himself and in his cause."

No virtue is merely personal : simply because human nature never stands by itself as a mere individual. Courage is essentially a personal virtue— the control of a man's fears by his higher nature : whether what is fearful be pains of body or of mind, loss of limb or life or of social reputation. But it is not merely personal : the call for these different kinds of control varies with their relation to social welfare, and divergent estimates of their value arise as social needs change. Thus, both to the Greek and to the Roman citizen military courage was the first article in the moral creed. The stability of the city depended on it ; tradition and custom demanded it as part of a citizen's outfit for life. Yet Plato saw that it was an imperfect expression of a man's nature. Mere soldiers, he said, tended to relapse into savagery, as mere men of science or scholars tended to degenerate in physical quality— till they became unable to maintain themselves in the struggle of life. He foresaw this as a danger which might result from the division of classes in his ideal state—the increasing rudeness of the military and weakness of the intellectual class : and he proposed to avoid the defects of both by blending the two strains in intermarriage.

The attitude of the early Christian converts showed a notable divergence from the antique model in reference to the courage which is the builder of cities and foster-mother of great races. They did not lack courage, even physical courage ; but it was in the way of bearing pain, oppression, and martyrdom ; it was endurance, fortitude. As for the more active courage of the warrior, or the enterprise of the statesman, it seemed to them energy misspent in service of a world which lay in wickedness, and the end of which was not far off. This changed moral attitude was undoubtedly a source of weakness to the Empire, many of the best of whose citizens learned to depreciate all worldly aims.

In the modern State there are other circumstances which may seem to lead to a decline in physical courage. Ease and luxury, wherever they abound, weaken the moral fibre and unfit a man to exert his powers to the full and to endure the shock of physical pain ; but ease and luxury are not peculiar to the newer civilisations. The whole tendency of the modern industrial system, however, has been thought to be unfavourable to the culture of physical courage. It accustoms men to a calling which, if not peaceful, at least settles its disputes by other means than force ; and where, as often happens in international relations, a peaceful settlement cannot be effected, the more commercial nations hire and set aside a special class—a standing army—to do their fighting for them.

Men of letters have lamented the decay of fighting quality ; and great soldiers have defended war as the training-ground of the noblest virtues : " without war," said von Moltke, " the world would deteriorate into materialism." It may be doubted, however, whether the effects of industrialism have been correctly analysed. Some five and thirty years ago, the late Walter Bagehot, a most acute and thoughtful observer, wrote as follows : " Somehow or other civilisation does not make men effeminate or unwarlike now as it once did. There is an improvement in our fibre—moral, if not physical. In ancient times, city people could not be got to fight—seemingly could not fight ; they lost their mental courage, perhaps their bodily nerve. But nowadays in all countries the great cities could pour out multitudes wanting nothing but practice to make good soldiers, and abounding in bravery and vigour. This was so in America ; it was so in Prussia ; and it would be so in England too. The breed of ancient times was impaired for war by trade and luxury, but the modern breed is not so impaired." The contrast is perhaps over-accentuated ; but there have been other instances, since Bagehot wrote, which might be quoted in support of his confident generalisation that trade has not weakened the fighting spirit of the race. " Somehow or other," courage of the ancient, heroic, physical kind has been preserved in modern character. And war is not the only condition that calls it forth. Courage of the same sort is required by the explorer and the inventor—by those who gather the material for science, and by those who apply its ideas for promoting human interests.

Further, modern life gains by recognising the wide extent of the virtue of courage—by finding it in regions, intellectual and philanthropic, where its presence was not clearly seen by ancient morality. It is especially in associating it with active devotion to the claims of truth and of benevolence that our conception has been widened. The man who endures toil and discouragement, danger or ridicule, in discovering and proclaiming truth, or in devoting his life to the service of others, displays a moral virtue essentially the same as that which the soldier shows in bearing the hardships of the campaign and the risks of battle,—and he displays the virtue on an even nobler field.

CHAPTER IV

It is difficult to assign the precise place of wisdom among the virtues. If we look simply to the excellent traits of human nature, there is nothing, we may say, more admirable than a wise and understanding soul. We would all make Solomon's choice, if we had the chance—or think we would. Yet we look upon wisdom as a gift, a brilliant quality, which is granted to some and denied to others, and which is entirely beyond our control. If virtue means simply excellence, then (with Aristotle) we call wisdom an intellectual virtue. But if we agree (as modern writers usually agree) to call by the name of virtue only those admirable qualities which are habits of will, and capable of voluntary modification, then we find difficulty in admitting it into our list.

If we are in earnest with this view of the nature of virtue, it seems clear that intellectual qualities, regarded merely as such, cannot be recognised as virtues at all. High qualities of intellect cannot properly be called virtues any more than distinguished physical capacities. In the Aristotelian ethics, we find science and art placed among the

virtues—and from one point of view correctly.
They are excellences of the intellect, just as strength
is an excellence of the bodily frame. But if virtue
is a volitional habit, then we cannot say that there
is a virtue of the man of science or of the artist, any
more than that there is a virtue of the strong man.
We shall have to say that the virtue depends on the
way in which natural qualities are cultivated and
applied under voluntary control.

Yet it is more than tradition which makes us
doubt whether our view of virtue would be complete
without definite recognition of an attitude of character which is to be regarded as primarily intellectual:
and if any place is assigned to this attitude then it
cannot be short of the highest. It may not com-
prehend all that common discourse and philosophy
have called by the name of wisdom, and it may
sometimes appear as if another name—truth or
sincerity, for example—would be more appropriate. Even with regard to temperance and
courage the denotation of the old terms has been
somewhat modified; and a like modification may be
permitted in the use of the term wisdom. Now, as
temperance may be called the virtue of the impulsive will, controlling and ordering the impulses
and desires, and as courage may be called the virtue
of the practical will, which disregards pain for the
sake of the object sought, so we want a name for the

virtue of the rational will, in which we find the highest manifestation of man's character—that which brings out his distinctive excellence as possessed both of reason and of freedom ; and for this purpose the word wisdom seems the fittest as it is the traditional term.

Again, the suitability of this way of regarding the matter may be seen if we revert to our initial view of the principle underlying the distinction among the personal virtues. The characteristics involved were said to be self-control and self-culture. The conception of self-control covered all that was meant by temperance. Courage was seen to occupy an intermediate place, involving on the one side control—the control of fear—and, on the other side, culture—the carrying out one's purpose. In the highest aspect of man's character, the element of subjection to control disappears. So far as man's will is completely rational, what is needed is culture only, not control by something else. Temperance, courage, and wisdom, therefore, may be taken to represent three stages or aspects of the virtuous character—the lowest, whose excellence consists in receiving due measure and purpose from the higher ; the intermediate, which requires both restraint and development ; and the highest, which gives unity and purpose to the whole nature, and aims at the realisation of its best capacities.

We have found the common characteristic of the virtues to lie in a state of will—a will in harmony with the good. The harmony may indeed be far from perfect ; but the more nearly it is approached, the higher is the virtue. Still further, we may be only faintly conscious of the nature of the good which is being realised in our own character. By instinct and training a man may show himself brave and his own master, without thinking much of the ends thereby achieved. Yet virtue is a state of consciousness— not mere instinct. It does not, of course, require elaborate reflection upon our own motives ; far less does it involve the morbid self-examination which turns life to bitterness. Its consciousness is not a consciousness of the individual self and its struggles and weaknesses, so much as a contemplation of, and firm hold on, the ideal self—the good which we approach in the very act of striving after it. From this point of view, the attitude which at once apprehends and wills the good is the root of all the virtues. This may be called the Good Will : and this good will realises itself in virtuous activities.

To say that this attitude is what is commonly meant by wisdom would be misleading, But it may be called the ground-plan of that virtue when understood as the excellence of the rational will. Its nature may become apparent by considering what it involves.

E

In the first place, take what may be called its *formal* aspect. The rational will, being rational, will not contradict itself. Facts will be faced as facts, principles recognised as principles. Our word wisdom means so much more that this aspect is apt to escape notice when we use the word. Truth or sincerity would be a better name. What is meant, however, is not so much truth in the communication of knowledge or information : that seems to be specially a social virtue, however closely connected with the present topic. It is truth as a feature of one's own consciousness and one's own outlook upon life. It is the truth to one's own self, from which it will follow that falsehood to another is impossible. However this may be, there can be no doubt of the pre-eminence in the virtuous character of sincerity or truth to oneself. In the words of R. L. Stevenson, ", Veracity to sentiment, truth in a relation, truth to your own heart and your friends, never to feign or falsify emotion—that is the truth which makes love possible and mankind happy." If we consider the matter fairly, we cannot fail to see how wide is the range, how subtle the influence of self-deceit. Not only do we often fear to face facts, we shrink from being confronted with ourselves. I do not say that we should be always inspecting ourselves, as if we were works of art that should hang on the wall, or subjects that should be laid out on the dissecting table. But knowledge of our own powers and purposes is the condition of effective activity. Conduct and character belong to consciousness ; virtue is a fact of consciousness ; and, if consciousness is untrue at its source, how can we expect purity in its result ? The Delphic oracle was right : the wise man must know himself.

This self-knowledge—or truth to self—reveals itself in our conduct as conscientiousness. If a question of duty arises we try to answer it in accordance with principle ; if we have to acquire knowledge, we seek to ascertain the facts and not merely what will suit our prejudices ; and in estimating reasonings we try to judge impartially, not to get arguments on our own side.

These, perhaps, are the chief formal aspects of this virtue of the rational will ; and, although they build upon certain given conditions of mind, yet they are all of them habits of volition, as much as courage is, or even temperance. They therefore belong to virtue in the modern sense. They are not the monopoly of the philosopher like the Platonic wisdom—nor do they involve a mode of activity freed altogether from desire such as Aristotle contemplated and sadly confessed to be too high for man. " If to be a true philosopher needs a greatness beyond the reach of the mere specialist student, yet to have the philosophic temper in a high degree—energy, modesty, the passion for truth, readiness to criticise ourselves—is within the reach of all who deal with ideas." But wisdom implies more than this merely formal aspect. To the latter, as already said, the name of truth may seem better suited. It is when we regard it as the supreme element in self-culture that the term wisdom becomes more appropriate. In its highest, and especially in its most intellectual, manifestations this culture of the reason can hardly be spoken of as within our power. We are forced to admit that it seems the possession of a select few, if indeed it be attainable at all in any perfection. Yet there are at least certain features of it which can be acquired by those who strive for them, however ordinary be their intellectual outfit : just as courage may be cultivated even by the man who can never rid himself of the physical shrinking of fear.

Conscientiousness and impartiality will lead to an effort after thoroughness in our understanding of the issues which we are called upon to meet. They will lead also to an attempt to select, from the infinite material presented in experience, those considerations which really bear on the issue. And it is on these characteristics — impartiality, thoroughness, and selection of the appropriate or important—that wise judgment in practical and even in intellectual matters mainly depends. Much more than these are, of course, needed to make a philosopher or man of science. But it is not laid upon everyone to unravel the mysteries of existence or extend the boundaries of knowledge. It is enough if he try to understand with a good conscience the part he is called upon to play in life. A well-known essayist has urged that " truth-hunting " may lead a man to neglect the ordinary moralities. No doubt it may. The essayist even suggests a preference for the question " What is trumps ? " over the question " What is truth ? " And one may admit that the former question is often more germane to the matter in hand. There is, indeed, a real temptation to fly off at a tangent from the sphere of one's own duties into the vague generalities which pass as first principles. A " man of sentiment " is not the type of perfect goodness. Nor, indeed, is he more than a mere caricature of rational virtue. The wise man is more apt to raise the question " Who is my neighbour ? " than the question " What is truth ? " The latter question is too often the expression of irony, or else of simple vacuity. Wisdom begins with what is before it—with consideration of oneself and one's circumstances : with " my station and its duties," we may say : and only on this basis does it build its superstructure, and attempt to understand life as a whole.

CHAPTER V

SOME OTHER PERSONAL VIRTUES

TEMPERANCE, courage, and wisdom have been called the virtues of the impulsive, the practical, and the rational will respectively. As such we may justly regard them as cardinal virtues, and as exhausting the cardinal virtues which are to be classed as personal rather than social. Other personal characteristics of the good man must be related to these : and concerning certain of them a word may be said.

Temperance, courage, and wisdom exhaust the leading qualities which, in Greek ethics, can be called personal virtues. If he possessed these, along with the social virtue of justice, a man was to be regarded as a good citizen ; he would perform such functions as the State required of him and for the rest enjoy his leisured life. The State would be only fulfilling its proper function if it provided the necessary leisure in which the philosopher might contemplate reality. The elegance and brilliancy of the life thus portrayed had also its dark side, only slightly concealed from view. It is borne in upon us as we read the ancient moralists that their ideal man, though he may undertake public service—fight for his

country and take his part in judicial and political
business—is yet never contemplated as under the
homely necessity of having to earn his own living.
The whole industrial fabric had as its foundation a
substructure of necessary work, which was looked
upon as beneath the dignity of the free citizen.
Plato and Aristotle did not write for the "labouring
poor," nor regard them as capable of the virtues
which they have recorded for all time as the praise
and glory of human character.   Their society was
based on slavery, and, without slaves, it would have
been impossible.   The bodily labour required by the
community was performed for the citizens either by
slaves or by artisans who were looked upon as doing
slaves' work, and thus as incapable of a citizen's
excellence.   If a citizen failed in courage on the field
of battle, if he avoided the claims made upon him
to serve in the magistracy or on the jury, he was
blamed for neglecting this civic duty.   But it would
have seemed absurd to the leading thinkers of the
times to assert—as we may now venture to do—that
INDUSTRY is an aspect of the virtue of the good
man.

The ancient virtue of courage contained within it
implicitly the basis of this more modern conception.
Its contempt of pain and danger involved persever-
ance in following a worthy purpose.   It was an
active virtue ; and yet the virtue of activity was

never fully recognised in the ancient view of courage. The highest life seemed to consist in leisured contemplation, and in the leisure almost as much as in the contemplation : so that the conception of self-culture on which the doctrine of virtue rests was not appreciated in its fullness.

That industry directed to a worthy end is an essential part of virtue is, in its clear statement, a modern, indeed a very modern idea. We have perhaps not yet got rid of the older idea that there are certain favoured families or classes into whose ideal development the necessity of work does not enter. At least our grandfathers, who had more respect for rank than their descendants have, favoured the idea. As evidence of this a passage may be quoted from the lessons in life with which that fine exponent of the old-fashioned aristocratic morality, Major Pendennis, instructed his nephew :

" ' Did you see that dark blue brougham, with that tremendous stepping horse, waiting at the door of the club ? You'll know it again. It is Sir Hugh Trumpington's ; he was never known to walk in his life ; never appears in the streets on foot—never. . . . He is now upstairs at Bays's, playing picquet with Count Punter ; he is the second-best player in England—as well he may be ; for he plays every day of his life, except Sundays (for Sir Hugh is an uncommonly religious man), from half-past three to half-past seven, when he dresses for dinner.'

" ' A very pious manner of spending his time,' Pen said, laughing. . . .

" ' Gad, sir, that is not the question. A man of his estate may employ his time as he chooses.' "

And in the previous century a much more exacting moralist than Major Pendennis—the severe Dr Johnson—snubbed his friend Boswell for reflecting on the frivolities of a lady of rank. " Sir," he said, " the Duchess of Northumberland may do what she pleases." Nor is this view restricted to one class or rank only. Labour is regarded as a curse not only by those who have no knowledge of it but also by those who have too much. From their point of view, we are told, " labour is an evil to be minimised to the utmost. The man who works at his trade or avocation more than necessity compels him, or who accumulates more than he can enjoy, is not a hero but a fool from the socialist's standpoint."

This view contrasts strangely with the encomiums often passed from similar quarters on the " dignity of labour." I venture to think that the latter conception has a truer ring, and is more in accordance with the conditions which have led to human progress. It is not by minimising labour, but by direct-

ing it to a noble end and elevating its conditions,
that the race can hope to attain a wiser, stronger,
purer manhood. The primeval curse has been made
the greatest agent of human progress. Let us read,
for example, Aristotle's typical description of leisured
virtue—the high-minded man, as he appeared to him,
possessing all the virtues and conscious of possessing
them, exacting the honour that is his due, neither
avoiding nor running into danger, ready to confer
but slow to accept a favour, holding aloof from all
enterprise except when great honour is to be won
by it, or a great work done, speaking the truth except
when he speaks ironically, pacing the streets with
slow and stately movement, and speaking, when he
speaks, in a deep voice and with measured utter-
ance, not in a hurry for there are few things in which
he is deeply interested, nor excited for he does not
hold anything to be of very great importance. There
are many points of contrast in this picture with the
modern ideal of virtuous manhood. And the cause
of many of the differences is the absence of any
function in the world, any continuous and fit work
to be performed by the Aristotelian high-minded
man. He seems to be merely ornamental, and even
as an ornament he offends our taste. Contrast with
this fancy portrait the real life of Spinoza support-
ing himself in humble independence by grinding
lenses, and devoting his thoughts to the elaboration

of the great idea of all things as in God.   Surely the
question need not be asked, which has the greater
dignity, which better represents the ideal of noble
manhood ?

The presence, in the modern conscience, of this
conception of the dignity of labour, and of industry
as an aspect of personal virtue, has been largely due
to the influence of the Christian view of mankind
as all under the same law, and to the assertion of
this equality of all men, in the form of a political
doctrine, by a long succession of moralists and jurists,
both in medieval and in modern times.

It would seem to be largely in connexion with
this political and economic influence that there has
been a tendency in some writers to restrict the
application of the virtue of industry in a way which
resembles the Aristotelian limitation of the extent
of the virtues of courage and temperance.   Industry
is interpreted as having to do solely with physical
work—the labour of one's hands, not of one's mind.
Thus in many Socialist utopias, from Sir Thomas
More to William Morris, the performance of a certain
number of hours' manual labour each day is made
compulsory on every citizen : a view which sharply
distinguishes these ideal commonwealths from the
Platonic state, in which function was adapted to
fitness, and manual labour in consequence restricted
to one class, and that the lowest.   This is not the

place to discuss the economic advantages and dis-
advantages of the provision favoured by some
socialists, that every citizen should perform a given
amount of manual labour. But the moral idea
which underlies it seems curiously perverted : for,
when it is required of everyone that, irrespective of
fitness for special kinds of work, he must perform
his own proportionate share in the physical work
which the community needs, we seem to be going
upon the underlying assumption that manual labour
is dignified if a man works for himself, but undigni-
fied if he is working for others. And this is a
paradox, which, in the mouths of those who maintain
the brotherhood of man, should rather be called a
blunder.

The primary kind of work is certainly manual
labour. Upon it as a basis all other kinds of work are
built. Further, it was the social necessity of the
labour of the hands that first led to emphasis being
laid on the importance of industry as a virtue of
character. " Some of the moralists of to-day," says
Professor J. S. Nicholson, " in their treatment of
labour questions, would do well to look back to the
medieval ideal. They would discover that many of
the noblest and most sympathetic of men—men who
showed their sympathy not in writing but in life-
long action—looked upon labour as an element of
duty and spiritual well-being ; they did not regard

it as degrading in itself or subversive of the higher morality, but rather as a healthy foundation of the spiritual life."

From the social point of view, however, it is more desirable that men should do what they are best fitted for, than that all men should do the same thing. And, from the individual's point of view, we have to remember that industry is simply the active side of personal virtue. It means the carrying out with system and energy the development of a man's powers, and their direction into worthy channels. The direction which should in each case be given to them cannot be foretold simply by consideration of the individual's own nature : here, as elsewhere, personal virtue merges in social.

The term Prudence is often used simply for practical wisdom. It was habitually employed in this sense by the medieval moralists. In ordinary discourse it seems to have only a less speculative and perhaps less dignified signification than wisdom. Thus we speak of a wise counsellor, but of a prudent father or prudent manager of an estate : though even here the usage has no established uniformity.

But there is another and different signification of the term prudence. Especially in English ethics, it is also used for what Butler called self-love—a rational and reflective regard for one's life—or happiness—on the whole : involving thus the restraint of impulses opposed to one's interest on the whole, and the cultivation of those natural tendencies which further one's interest.

Of prudence in the former sense enough has been said in dealing with the virtue of wisdom. But of prudence in the latter sense, the question has been asked whether it should be regarded as a virtue or not ; and to that question a short consideration may be devoted.

Butler says that prudence, that is to say, " a due concern about our own interest or happiness," is " a species of virtue." In so saying, he is thinking of self-love or prudence as a " calm reflective principle " by which the rush and storm of the passions may be quieted and guided, and which is never really inconsistent with benevolence. It is a rational principle, superior to the various particular impulses, and clearly vested with authority over them ; and it is the rational nature of the quality which makes Butler give it so high a place.

On the other hand Kant looked to its end, which is the interest of the self merely, or, in other words, personal happiness. Now Kant sometimes surprises us in his treatment of this notion of happiness, which is indeed the centre of many perplexities in ethics. He does not, as his general attitude might have led us to expect, deny that it is of any moral worth whatever. In our social or extra-regarding activities, happiness, that is the happiness of others, is the only end, he says, for a man to aim at ; but, with regard to one's own happiness, there is no ethical value in deliberately directing our conduct to that end. Perhaps his decision is in this case correct ; but the reason he gives for it is certainly wrong. He thinks that nature has so ordered our impulses that of themselves they lead us to our own greatest happiness ; that the interference of our reason in the matter is impertinent and confusing— as if we could teach nature how best to attain its end. Nature itself always takes the best course. Kant, however, like so many thinkers of his day, was misled by one of the dominant errors of the time —a belief in the perfection of nature as a system of means and ends. He forgot that man's reason is certainly—to say the least—not more imperfect than his instincts and impulses ; and that, although his reason may often err, nature acting through his impulses still more often and obviously leads him astray.

It appears to me, on the whole, that prudence is a virtue. I should define it as the habit of controlling the impulses and desires of the moment with a view to the interests of the individual life as a whole. It is, therefore, a case of the bringing of rational order into the region of immediate feeling and impulse. But it is a virtue short of the highest—short of the temperance guided by wisdom —in so far as its end or purpose is restricted to a view of the individual life and its interests.

If we interpret " interests " from a merely hedonistic point of view—if it is only for pleasure to come, that pleasure of the moment is controlled— are we not, as Plato said, simply temperate for the sake of intemperance ? We have sufficient control not to be the sport of each passing appetite and desire ; but we put them aside only for a more deliberate and long drawn-out gratification in the future. Prudence owes its rank as a virtue to the fact that this narrow interpretation of interests is not commonly met with outside the pages of the hedonistic philosopher.

Again, if the restriction to the individual life and its interests be so interpreted as to emphasise those points in which individual interest is apt to be opposed to social welfare, then the life may be higher than the life of mere impulse, inasmuch as it is more deliberate and rational, but, at the same time, it may be more dangerous to the health of the social organism. It is because the individual does not stand alone, and his interests usually draw the interests of others after them, that we give prudence a place, uncertain though it may be, among the virtues. The place is uncertain simply because the end in view, which determines the nature of the virtue, is so conceived as to be short of the highest end and even liable to be turned to unworthy purposes. It has the form of virtue because it involves the rule of the lower by the higher; but its moral worth depends on the degree in which its purpose or end is free from selfishness and from pleasure-seeking.

The much-lauded virtue of THRIFT is simply prudence applied to the management of income or wealth : provision for the future taking the place of immediate expenditure. We may call it a virtue in so far as it postpones present pleasure to the interest and well-being of the life as a whole, and in so far as it is—as it commonly is—for the sake of others, as well as for one's own sake, its worth is higher. But it is a virtue which often shivers on the brink of vice, as when it prevents the spending of money for a worthy object, or represses the social virtue of liberality.

There is no contradiction in this. We must not be misled by names, or by the abstract ideas which names signify. Thrift is the name for a mental habit, and may be given to different mental habits owing to the similarity of the conduct proceeding from them—to wit, saving money. But the moral quality depends on the purpose in view in the action

F

It has been said, by a writer already quoted, that
Socialism " is radically at variance with thrift " ;
and a labour leader, ignorant of the responsibilities
which the future had in store for him, once asserted
that " thrift was invented by capitalist rogues to
beguile fools to destruction, and to deprive honest
fools of their diet and their proper comfort." He
did not explain how capitalists ever could have come
into being before thrift was " invented " ; nor why
the man who has put aside a portion of his wages
is less able to cope with the " capitalist rogue " than
the man who has spent every farthing. But there
is often a grain of truth in a bushel of oratorical
absurdity. Thrift may be a very sordid selfish virtue
—that is, no virtue at all. From the moral point
of view everything depends on the motive or purpose.
It makes all the difference whether present enjoyment is subordinated to secure the future means of
a worthy life—this is a virtuous habit ; or whether
generous impulses are stifled, lest one lose perfect cer-
tainty of having all the means of enjoyment at hand
in one's own future. The latter is like the " vulgar
compound of temperance and niggardly earthly ways
and motives " spoken of by Plato. It " will breed
meanness in your inmost soul, although it is praised
by the vulgar as virtue, and will send you bowling
round the earth during a period of nine thousand
years, and leave you a fool in the world below."

When Sir Walter Eliot, in Jane Austen's novel, was forced to consider the necessity of retrenchment, the first suggestions that occurred were to cut off some subscriptions to public objects and *not* to bring Anne a present from London. This is one kind of thrift. But it is not the same thing to the moralist whether thrift begins in restricting one's luxuries or in cutting off one's charities.

In thrift, as in every other personal quality, we must look to the end. Its value lies in the relief it offers from the pressing cares of mere living, and the scope it gives for the higher life. The common wants of life have to be supplied before free play can be given to the activities which raise man above the level of animal existence ; and the fear of want is apt to keep the faculties on the strain merely for the sake of living and the making of a livelihood. This fear must be mastered—reduced at least to a subordinate place in life—to make possible the higher culture in which true excellence consists. There are many favoured beings to whom the fear has never presented itself in its grim reality, to whom the comforts and conveniences of living come without a thought. But it is not so with the great majority of men. Their lives may be wholly taken up in providing the means of living, and without ever being quite secure of these means. Work and wages are often the sport of circumstances over which the workman has no control. A new invention, a change of fashion, a trade dispute, may force him to " begin life " anew ; sickness may disable him from work ; and if he escape these, old age lies before, when he must fall out of the ranks. Either he must take no thought for the morrow at all, or the fear of want will dog his steps and sit a spectre at his board. The spectre may be exorcised by the homely quality of thrift, in which a portion of the gains of industry is set aside as an insurance against its uncertainty. In this way industry is made to provide the remedy for its own evils ; and the prudent man foresees these evils and uses the remedy. The advantage he gains does not lie only or chiefly in the provision against want when sickness or old age actually comes upon him ; it has not been lost though he die suddenly in full work ; its chief value lies in the security which it gives to his whole life : it raises him above the most pressing and depressing fears ; it gives the consciousness of independence ; it liberates his interests, and sets free his activities in the direction of mental culture and social service. It is only when his soul is in the savings-bank, as well as his coin, that the vicious tendency in thrift appears. Then a man's thoughts and purposes are centred in his own personal security from poverty ; in fighting it, he magnifies the fear of it, and becomes its slave : he

checks desire lest it diminish this security ; he
hardens his heart because even sympathy may
become expensive ; he limits his interests lest they
be a drain upon his savings ; and thus there is produced—even on this side miserliness—the unlovely
type of the thrifty man, who guards his small earn-
ings with jealous care, and is stingy to himself as
well as to others—a hard man, just but ungenerous,
paying strictly all his legal dues, and contriving that
they shall be as small as possible, but forgetful of the
great debt of human brotherhood, and treating life
as a commercial account which has been well lived
if the books show a balance at the end.   On the
other hand the thriftless man may be full of generous
impulses and of noble sentiments ; open-handed
and large-hearted, he has often the qualities which
call forth affection, and his failings seem pardonable
compared with the defects which are apt to go along
with the meanest of the virtues.

CHAPTER VI

JUSTICE

ALL the virtues have important social bearings. Some of them may even owe the special form they take to social conditions. Courage, for example, though its essence remains the same, manifests itself in very different ways according as the surrounding circumstances are the dangers of a military campaign or the stifling intellectual atmosphere of some little social clique.

But certain virtues have their direct origin in man's position as a social being and would not arise at all—could not be thought of—if man were not a member of a community. Temperance, courage, and wisdom can all have a certain (though inadequate) meaning given to them by considering man as if he were a solitary being. They will find scope in the discipline and development of his personal character. But no meaning at all can be given to justice or benevolence which does not involve the conception of other persons and their relation to the individual. By the social virtues therefore we mean those habits of personal character —for it is still personal character with which we

deal—which exhibit the moral attitude of the individual as a member of a community, and which
have meaning regarding him only in that social
relation. And just as the personal virtues were
said to be concerned with the due ordering of the
lower by the higher nature of man, so the social
virtues exhibit the due attitude of a man to other
persons or to the social whole.

The social virtues must obviously be closely
related to the special conditions of social order
existing at any time : apart, on the one side, from
an historical account of some particular civilisation,
and, on the other hand, without entering upon a
complete social philosophy, it is very difficult to
determine the nature and scope of the fundamental
or cardinal virtues of the social man. In all accounts
justice holds a foremost place, if it does not indeed
exhaust the whole field. But justice seems always
to have relation to the recognition of definite rights
on the part of others and to be limited to due
regard for these rights. A more positive and more
generous attitude towards others demands recognition in the constitution of the moral life. The
classical moralists of Greece never met this demand
fully. In Aristotle's ethics, indeed, there are many
suggestions of the larger view of social morality : in
his description of the virtuous attitude towards the
spending of one's means, giving the virtues of

liberality and magnificence, and in the minor virtues which he includes in his list and which have to do with the amenities of social intercourse, but most of all in his discourses on friendship. To the Stoics a far deeper conception is due. By their day, the chains of the aristocratic constitution of Athenian life had been broken, and the unity of the human race first appealed to them with living force and led to their recognition of the virtue of benevolence—which, afterwards, under the name of charity or love, was held by Christian writers to express the sum and substance of all the virtues.

We may look upon justice and benevolence as the fundamental social virtues ; and the reasons for doing so will be made clearer as their nature is exhibited. Their distinction from one another has been aptly indicated by defining justice as the principle of giving a citizen his due, and benevolence as the principle of seeking his good as a man. These, of course, are merely formal definitions, for they leave undetermined the questions, What is a citizen's due ? and What is his good as a man ? But they give a preliminary point of view from which these questions may be attacked.

A history of the views of moralists concerning justice would be almost the same thing as a history of moral and political philosophy. The question of what is due from man to man in virtue of his manhood and citizenship raises or touches almost every question in ethics. And it is not easy to give, in short compass, any intelligible account of that aspect of virtuous character. It is so comprehensive and yet so subtle that moralists are agreed in almost nothing about it except in calling it justice.

An initial difficulty arises from a confusion. Justice, in almost every meaning given to the term, has something to do with law. And as the laws may be supposed to cover the whole field of the moral life, and do, as a matter of fact, concern almost all kinds of conduct, there is a sense in which justice may seem to be co-extensive with the whole of moral virtue. This was especially the case in certain ancient societies, such as the Greek city-states. In them the just man might have been said to be the law-abiding man : including, perhaps, under " law," not merely the explicit edicts of the sovereign power, but also the normal expectations which were formed about conduct by social opinion and which were, to some extent, backed up by its sanctions. In this sense the just man is the same as the righteous man of Scripture, whose characteristic was that he kept the whole law, therein regarded as the divine law and therefore as leaving no moral duty outside its scope.

But it is not with this universal justice (as Aristotle called it) that we are concerned. We give the name justice to a special aspect of the moral life ; we distinguish it not only from temperance and courage and wisdom, but also from benevolence ; and it is into this special excellence of character that we have to inquire.

There is a branch of justice which has to do with the putting right of wrongs. It is this branch which bulks most largely in our eyes ; and to it what are called Courts of Justice are restricted, or almost entirely restricted. Historically also, it would seem to be the aspect of justice which finds earliest expression in the human conscience. It is wrongs—offences against rights—which first bring rights to consciousness ; and it is in connexion with wrongs that the germ of justice first shows signs of life in our instinctive or impulsive nature.

There is a hint of this view in Aristotle in a passage in which he speaks of *nemesis* as the natural source or impulsive basis of justice : though he does not work out the view or even mention it in his express and elaborate treatment of the virtue. He points out that the sense of shame may be taken as the first instinctive appearance of temperance, and that in the same way the feeling of *nemesis*, that is, indignation or resentment, is the seed in human nature out of which the virtue of justice grows.

The term *nemesis* has, however, from the first,

a certain moral connotation and is so treated
by Aristotle.   It is righteous indignation, and
means " distribution of what is due," while it was
personified as the goddess of justice from whom
retribution comes.   Leaving out of sight this moral
implication for the moment—for indeed it seems
hardly present at the start—we may look upon
indignation or resentment as the instinctive germ
of justice.   The impulse which stirs us to ward off a
hurt from ourselves, and which prompts to retaliation and revenge, is a tendency which, when moralised, leads us to the very heart of what we mean
by justice.

Thus Bacon begins his famous essay on revenge
with the words " Revenge is a kind of wild
justice."   He looks upon it therefore as a sort of
rival to official or legal justice, and as needing
accordingly all the greater restraint by law : " The
more a man's nature runs to [revenge], the more
ought law to weed it out.   For as for the first wrong
it doth but offend the law ; but the revenge of that
wrong putteth the law out of office."

In this passage Bacon writes as a lawyer, not,
certainly, as an historian of custom.   Revenge exists
before law.   And it does not disappear when law
arises, partly because it is a tendency which has
been organised in the human constitution and can
only gradually be displaced, partly because law does

in a regular way and on principle a part only of what revenge does or desires.

An illustration of the close connexion between law and this natural feeling of resentment is afforded by a theory put forward by certain eminent jurists. They have looked upon the criminal law, which punishes offences, as a means of giving a regulated satisfaction to the natural feeling of resentment and desire for revenge. The view is interesting ; but I do not think that it is sound. It confuses the purpose of law and legal penalties with their historical origin. Legal penalties are not now inflicted on the wrong-doer because the man who has suffered the wrong desires to see him in pain ; but because it has been discovered both that the pain which the injured man would himself have inflicted in his own wild way serves the moral or social purpose of preventing wrong, and also that this is an end which can be still better secured if the penalty be determined and inflicted by the organised force of society instead of being left to the caprice or passion of the injured man.

The instinct of revenge—at any rate before it had come in contact with, and been modified by, legal methods—seems careless alike of individual responsibility and of the intentional character of the injury. In the earliest forms of historical societies, resentment is not directed solely against the person who has done the wrong ; his whole kith and kin are involved in the offence and liable to pay the penalty to the injured man and his family. Both wrong and resentment are looked upon as not personal but tribal. Early hostility is a blood-feud, and a remnant of this form of social order still survives in the vendetta of semi-civilised races. Nor does the intention with which the original act was performed make any difference. To the passion of resentment hurt and wrong are the same, and are equally followed by the desire for retaliation. It is only after reflection, and in the course of the organisation of social life, that personal responsibility is fixed, and the intention of an act taken into account. " The soul that sinneth *it* shall die." These words stand for a revolution in the moral ideas of the race. They mark the beginning of civilised morality and the basis of civilised law. The responsibility for an act is limited to the agent who performed it ; and the degree of his responsibility is made to depend on his intention in the act, as distinguished from the accidental or external circumstances which may have modified it.

If a purchaser is charged thirty shillings for an article which is ticketed in the shop-window at one pound, there is unfairness in the transaction, and he has been wronged. Accordingly he will have a claim for the return of ten shillings ; and this return will restore the bargain to fairness in accordance with the shopkeeper's contract with the public. If the overcharge was due to accident or oversight, there is no more to be said. But if there was deliberate deception on the salesman's part, then it becomes a case of fraud ; modern civilisation takes cognisance of it under the criminal law and punishment is inflicted. In either case—whether the unfairness of the transaction was due to oversight or to deliberate deception —we start with a wrong which needs to be redressed or righted. And, logically, this conception of a wrong done implies the conception of a right that has been violated : although the latter conception may have emerged later in the historical development of moral ideas. The fundamental question for the theory of justice, therefore, concerns the nature of rights : it is only when the rights of an individual or of the society have been violated that the question of redress arises ; it is only when they have been intentionally violated that the punishment of the offender can have moral justification.

It is natural that the question of justice should most prominently suggest to us the redress of wrongs and the punishment of offenders. That is what a man is commonly thinking of when justice is his plea, or when he goes into court seeking for justice.

But logically justice must be concerned with rights before it can decide upon wrongs. And the just man may accordingly be described as the man in whom respect for the rights of others has become a habit of will. The meaning and extent of justice will therefore depend on the account we are able to give of what are called the " rights " of man.

Here, then, we are face to face with the real difficulty of the question. The just man is the man into whose volitional nature there is ingrained a habit of respecting the rights of others. What are those rights ?

The first and most obvious answer is that a man's rights are the things which the law secures to him by preventing interference with them by others. He has a right to his property, that is, the law will punish persons who steal it from him. He has a right to liberty, that is, the law will punish anyone who puts restraint upon his person. He has a right to his good name : there is a law of libel for anyone who calumniates him. His rights are other people's duties—duties which the law sanctions by punishing their violation. The just man then, it may be said, is the person whose cultivated habit of will leads him to obey this law without the compulsion of its penalties, who, freely and from trained volitional habit, respects the legal rights of others. This is an important feature of his character, but clearly it is not all. A riparian proprietor might reasonably accuse his up-river neighbour of interfering with his rights if he polluted the stream that was to pass by his house—and his attitude would be reasonable even if there were no law against the pollution of rivers. He would contend that he had a right which ought to be respected, even although no law enforced it. He would be contending for a moral right, therefore. The gradual modification of legal rights nearly always follows in the wake of some such view of moral rights. Again, we should call a man unjust if, without good cause, he were to disinherit his eldest and youngest sons for the advantage of his second son. We recognise a right on the part of the other sons to a share in the inheritance, although no such right is admitted by English law. Ordinary social opinion, however, sanctions the claim, and ordinary social practice leads to a certain normal expectation of conduct corresponding to the practice. We say that the rights of the eldest and youngest sons were violated, because their normal expectations were disappointed.

The just man, it might therefore seem, respects not merely legal rights but also normal expectations. Yet such normal expectations are often without the clear and precise outlines which we desiderate in the distinction of justice from injustice. Besides, we are willing to admit that these normal expectations should not always be encouraged and perpetuated. Otherwise, social arrangements would be stereotyped, and reform would become impossible. Certain expectations corresponding to rights of fundamental importance are essential to the well-being of society. But where there is a strong compelling force requiring everything to be done as one's neighbours expect it to be done, social progress is hindered. The wider the sweep of these normal expectations and the stronger the sanctions which defend them, the less progressive is the society. They characterise eastern rather than western social methods, and in the west, the life of the village rather than the life of the town. The less progressive the community the greater is the displeasure with which what is called eccentricity, either of thought or conduct, is visited, and the less room is there for individual freedom. Justice, no doubt, represents the permanent and relatively fixed aspect of social life—the aspect of order rather than that of progress—but it cannot consist in an attitude which is essentially obstructive of progress. It is, therefore, not a sufficient account of the just man's character—though it contains a portion of the truth—to say that he is a respecter of the rights of others as fixed by law or by the opinion and customs of the society of the time. We may take this, if we like, as expressing what has been called the Conservative

G

element in justice. The term " just," meaning this
conformity to "what is required," has sometimes
been used in an unfavourable sense, and even as a
term of dispraise, in which justice is opposed to
generosity. But a larger view of human rights
makes this usage less applicable. We hardly call
that employer, for instance, just who only pays his
men their wages and holds that he has no duties to
them beyond those which the law enforces. The
just man may observe the rights sanctioned by
society, but he will respect others also of which the
society is careless, and he may attempt to modify
the social standard by an appeal to what may be
called Ideal Justice.

We cannot get a satisfactory account of justice
without taking this ideal element into consideration. We have to include not only the rights
which are enforced by law or social opinion, but
also others varying more or less from these, which
we have ground for saying *ought* to belong to men.

A theory of what is called Natural Rights has
thus been worked out in this connexion. And it is
characteristic of this theory that the rights claimed
are held to be independent of positive or historical
enactment. These natural rights—so the exponents
of the theory contend—belong to men irrespective
of all social institution : and societies and legal

systems are good or bad according to the measure
in which they recognise them.

A very long list might be made of such rights as
they have been claimed and expounded by one *a
priori* philosopher or another. Some idea of them
may be given by a partial and classified enumeration.

First comes the right to Life : which is sometimes
made to involve a right to work—and to have work
provided for one—in order that life may be maintained ; sometimes also, to include a right to
happiness, in order that life may be worth maintain-
ing. Secondly, there is the right to Property (defined
as the produce direct or indirect of one's labour),
which is usually held to include the right to use one's
property, to prevent others from using it, and to
destroy it ; and the right to alienate it whether by
exchange, by gift, or by bequest. Thirdly, there is
the right to Freedom, which has many meanings and
applications : such as, in the first place, freedom of
thought : to hold one's own opinion and to convince
others of it by speech or print ; in the second place,
freedom of action, as in choosing one's business, in
entering into contracts, and in employing one's
leisure ; in the third place, freedom of combination
along with others for the achievement of any lawful
purpose ; in the fourth place, perhaps, freedom to
resist oppression, that is, the right to rebel if the
ruling power of society interferes with one's rights ·

and, in the fifth place, under the name of the franchise, a share in the government, or in electing representatives in the government, is regarded as the mark of a citizen of a free country. Fourthly, there is the right to have the contracts made with one fulfilled, and generally to Good Faith. And fifthly, there is the right to Equality, including, in the first place, impartial treatment by the law, and, in the second place, impartial treatment in the distribution of the benefits of life.

This is a large Bill of Rights; and, as a matter of fact, no community has ever recognised them all without qualification. This may appear unimportant seeing that they are ideals. They do not claim to be legal rights, but rather natural rights which a perfect law would observe. They claim ideal validity only. But, even as regards this claim, it must be pointed out that no system of laws could maintain them all, for they are not consistent with one another. If we are to recognise an inherent or natural right to life, it can only be by making large restrictions upon the right to property; and if we are to establish a right to happiness, the problem is graver still, and indeed impossible of solution. Again, the right to have a contract fulfilled is itself a limitation of the abstract right to freedom, for it limits the freedom of one of the parties to the contract. And the right to equality is not only vague in statement, but each step taken to realise it involves some interference with the abstract right to freedom. In short, if we define the just man as the man who respects all these so-called natural rights, we make his nature a rubbish shoot for all the contradictions and generalities of *a priori* politics.

The fallacy of the doctrine of natural rights lies in the independent validity assigned to each one of the so-called rights. These all describe—in very general terms, it is true, and perhaps not very accurately— certain factors of the social order, at least, of any desirable social order. Such an order seeks to realise life and liberty, an equal law and stable industrial system in the best possible way. It is when we treat each factor as of the nature of an absolute indefeasible right that contradictions enter, and we find the system will not work. Accordingly, theorists have sought for some leading idea to which all the others may be subordinated ; and in this way two rival views of ideal justice have been elaborated, corresponding to the two leading ideas in the group of natural rights—Liberty and Equality.

These are rival ideas. Yet the two always went together in older doctrines of natural rights. That all men were free and equal was a characteristic of the supposed state of nature, antecedent to every political constitution, which was a leading idea with medieval and many modern political philosophers.

When actual laws and institutions seemed oppressive, the characteristics of this imaginary state of nature came to be regarded as the goals of revolutionary progress, as " rights " of which men had been too long deprived by tyranny. It was thought that the ideal state would be established or restored, and the long grievance of humanity remedied, when a new order of freedom and equality had taken the place of the old order of restraint and privilege.

The results, so far, of the preceding pages may now be summed up, before an attempt is made to determine more precisely the nature of justice. Justice is the volitional habit which disposes a man to respect the rights of others. It is thus essentially a social virtue : the term has no meaning apart from the relation of the person called "just" to other persons who are regarded as having " rights." Accordingly, we cannot understand what is meant by " justice " until we can give a meaning to this term " rights." Every community, however, recognises certain rights as belonging to its members ; and, in the modern state, the rights of citizens are defined and enforced by law. This gives us a clue in our search for an explanation of the meaning of rights. Yet we have found that legal rights do not exactly coincide with moral rights. Moral rights may exist without the sanction of law ;

and the law may admit a right which morality re-
fuses to recognise. If the two were coincident, the
virtue of justice would find its complete realisation
in law-observance ; and we should be unable to
explain the obvious fact that laws themselves—as
well as social customs and normal expectations—
are constantly being tested and amended by the
application of some moral or ideal standard. This
ideal standard was, for long, identified with a certain
doctrine of indefeasible rights which were supposed
to belong to every man by nature, and which it was
the business of social institutions to manifest and
confirm. These so-called natural rights were not
often enumerated completely ; nor did their exponents show how all of them could be realised at
the same time. But stress was laid chiefly upon
two of them—liberty and equality. These were
commonly regarded as companion, not as rival, ideals ;
but they have led to two different theories as to
the nature of justice and of social order generally.

Kant and Herbert Spencer may be instanced as
having used the conception of liberty for the purpose
of defining the meaning of justice. They agreed
also in interpreting liberty in a negative way as
equivalent simply to freedom from interference.
The essence of justice is made to consist in non-
interference ; and a state is regarded as realising
justice in its legal system when every citizen is

left free to act as he will provided that he does not
by his action interfere with the like freedom of others.
To be made effective this view has to be supplemented by a distinction between those actions of
a man which do not and those which do affect
others in such a way as may limit their freedom.
These two spheres of his activity must be delimited ;
and, if this can be done, we may call the two spheres
self-regarding acts and other-regarding acts respectively ; and it will then be possible to maintain
that self-regarding acts should be left to each man's
choice, whereas the organised control of the state
should regulate other-regarding acts so that they
may not limit the freedom of others ; the just state
will make laws enforcing this result, and the just
man will observe these laws, without feeling their
constraint, for they will have become in him a
trained habit of will. The thinkers who adopt this
view set very definite limits to the functions of the
state ; these limits are designed to safe-guard the
freedom of the individual; and the political theory
which results is known as Individualism.

Other writers have fixed upon equality as the
fundamental constituent of ideal justice. The conception of equality, indeed, enters in some degree
into every doctrine of justice ; justice has to do
with what is fair or equal as between man and man ;
and the strictest individualist recognises this in

claiming equal freedom for all men. But there are
other elements of value in life besides freedom ; and
when equality is claimed in respect of them, a different doctrine results. It takes many forms according to the kind of equality in view ; and its extreme
form would be a communism which required an
equal distribution of all the goods of life. Socialism
does not make this demand ; but the ethical idea
which underlies the socialist doctrine of justice is
the idea of equality. It should be added, however, that in recent expositions of the creed, chief
emphasis is laid on the social organisation and
control required, and the idea of equality becomes
less prominent and, sometimes, almost disappears.

Take, in the first place, the view of justice which
is founded on the idea of liberty—interpreted as
meaning non-interference. No one has been able
to unfold the meaning of this idea in a systematic
and consistent way and at the same time to make
it describe a social order which can be called just.
It has been supported by a distinction between self-
regarding and other-regarding activities, non-interference being claimed only for the former. Even
if the distinction could be drawn satisfactorily, the
problem would still remain, for it is with social
conduct that justice is concerned. But conduct of
every kind has social effects and may thus tend to
limit the freedom of other men. Even the expression

of a man's views influences the opinions of others ; the property he acquires takes away their freedom to obtain the same things ; in some industrial conditions the wages offered by an employer may leave the workmen free only to accept his terms or to starve ; in certain circumstances even this alternative may not be left open ; and the result is arrived at in the name of freedom.

Historical development, especially in industrial affairs, has made plain the conclusion that the extension of liberty, in the sense of non-interference, does not promote human equality. The first thing needful may have been to assert individual freedom against the interference and tyranny of the government. The history of freedom has two aspects, constitutional and personal. Constitutional or political freedom is realised when the government of a country adequately represents the will of the people ; personal freedom is realised when the government, however constituted, does not interfere unduly in their lives. Personal freedom has been most strongly asserted—as it has been most frequently restricted—in the two spheres of religion and industry. In questions of belief the gospel of liberty was preached, in times of revolution, by Milton and John Locke ; and their pleas for toleration triumphed. The prophet of industrial freedom was Adam Smith. In a historical review of the progress of opulence he showed how trade had been turned out of its most beneficial channels by the unwise regulations of governments ; he held that, if traders were left to pursue their own interests in their own way, the greatest advantage to the community would result ; he recommended the removal of restrictions, and trusted to the " simple system of natural liberty." In course of time his ideas bore fruit ; one by one the old restrictions on trade were abolished ; natural liberty was allowed to work out its natural results. Some of these results were obvious and beneficial ; but it was only gradually that observers began to note that the promotion of equality was not one of them. Natural liberty accentuated inherent inequalities, and seemed to lead to a greater difference of condition than had existed before between rich and poor, employer and employed, educated and uneducated.

Gradually, therefore, men came under the influence of a new order of ideas ; and nearly all the important legislation of the last generation or more has tended in the direction not of liberty, but of equality. And the result has been more quickly apparent than in the former case ; it is seen that each step towards equality has involved some limitation of the individual freedom which was formerly claimed as the natural right of man.

We are still far from the end of this progress in

the direction of equality.   And confidence as to
all its results would be premature. Yet we are
able to see that when an attempt is made to render
precise the idea of equality, it had various competing meanings ; and it also becomes clear that
it is not possible, from any one of these, to derive
a satisfactory definition of justice.

Equality might be so interpreted as to mean
simply equality before the law ; but equality of this
sort was always admitted as desirable even under
the régime of unlimited freedom.   There is nearly
always present, however, as there is always required,
a provision that the laws themselves should be equal,
that is just ; and in the interpretations of what
belongs to a just or equal law, all the old difficulties
reappear.   Again, it might be contended that what
is wanted is equality of opportunity.   But this view
would require us to fix some arbitrary point as the
end of the individual's training or education, up to
which point all individuals should be dealt with
equally, and after which they should be given a
perfectly fair start in the race for life and for the
goods of life.   When the difficulty of fixing this
point had been surmounted, we should only be in
presence of a competition, somewhat fairer at the
start than the older system, but sown with the
seeds of greater bitterness and contention, for in it
the weaker competitors would have to endure a

harder fate than under the present system.   Equality
of opportunity, therefore, with competitors unequal
as they are, would only accentuate differences ; it
would not give nor tend to a real equality of conditions.   Hence the demand for tempering the inequalities which result from private enterprise can
only be satisfied by establishing some measure of
equality in the distribution of goods.   Even here,
however, we are not at an end of ambiguities.   For
arithmetical equality is seldom demanded.   It would
not only need a fresh redistribution on the occasion
of each birth and each death in the human family ;
but it would require the assignment of equal shares
to child and man, irrespective of their needs or
deserts.   It is therefore, almost always allowed
that the equality required must be interpreted as
some kind of proportion.   But proportion to what ?
Entirely different social orders will result according
as we make our standard that of social welfare, and
distribute goods in proportion to social efficiency ;
or as we adopt a personal standard ; and then the
division will be altogether different according as
we take effort or need as the ground upon which
each man's share is to be determined.   If effort
were taken as the standard, we should require
omniscience to determine it ; and if need were taken
as the standard, then the stimulus to industry would
be removed and the moral element eliminated from

the rewards of industry, so that, whatever else our
socialistic state might be, it would not be a just state.

Justice therefore, it would seem, cannot consist
either in abstract freedom or in abstract equality.
And the ideals are antagonistic. Equality is gained
only by constant interferences with liberty. And
liberty, conceived in this abstract fashion, has been
shown to be hostile to the realisation of equality :
of real equality, of equality of opportunity, and
even of equality before the law, wherever (as in
this country) legal proceedings are expensive.

If the conception of liberty is of so little avail
in assisting us to determine the nature of the just
man or of the just state, it may be because the conception is almost entirely negative. It has been
interpreted as meaning simply non-interference,
absence of restraint. Thus the question arises
whether liberty is necessarily a merely negative
conception ; whether its meaning is exhausted by
non-interference or whether it may be possible to
give positive content and thereby also ethical value
to the conception. If this can be done, we shall
have to enlarge the meaning of the conception so
as to include freedom to develop or cultivate one's
nature as a moral being. This wider conception
will thus involve both negative freedom from interference, or rather, as we ought to say, from undue

interference, and also positive freedom ; and positive
freedom will imply the presence of those conditions
without which freedom from interference is worthless;
that is, it will include the means and opportunities of
realising one's personal and social capacities.

Undoubtedly, this seems a worthier social ideal
than either abstract liberty or abstract equality.
But it is also vague ; and when we attempt to make
clear what it involves, no little want of precision still
remains.

The ideal of Positive Freedom would seem to
involve the following conditions.   In the first place,
the development and direction of mental and
physical powers by education.   In the second place,
as education only fits a man for work and does not
provide him with the necessary means therefor, the
ideal would seem to involve certain industrial
factors, namely, access to the materials and instruments of production.   These need not necessarily
be assigned absolutely to the individual, nor need
the whole product be regarded as his private property ; but such access to industrial material and
instruments would be required as would give suitable
employment : calling forth the industry, intelligence,
and special gifts of a man, and followed by suitable
reward.   In the third place, physical and social surroundings should be provided so as to aid and not
to hamper individual development.

It is thus clear that the ideal of positive freedom contains a great deal more than freedom in any ordinary meaning of the term. It involves, also, a wholesale restriction of the liberty claimed by the older or individualist writers. To carry it out, it would be necessary to restrict the negative liberty of some in order to provide the means essential to the development of others ; and it would also be necessary to restrict the liberty of these others in many ways, so as to prevent them from accepting conditions of work or of life opposed to their own development or to social welfare. And these restrictions, it would further appear, tend to bring the ideal of positive freedom into closer connexion with equality, but without making the latter into an absolute rule.

It must be admitted, also, that positive freedom, as thus conceived, is of the nature of an ideal. The various elements implied in it have been indicated, and even this general statement of them shows them to be large and far reaching : access to industrial instruments, suitable employment, scope for realising a full human life. These cannot be formulated as definite rights for all or any particular time. Otherwise, moral rights would be the same as moral needs ; if we define justice as consisting in respect for these as the rights of all men, then justice is indistinguishable from benevolence. If we would have a definition of justice which is not limited to a far-off, perhaps unattainable, ideal, and wish to describe the character of the just man as he appears in various historical surroundings, we must be content with some much less elaborate description of the rights which he respects in others. In the case of justice, as in the case of temperance and of courage, there has been a gradual widening of men's views of the application of the virtue. When we say that the just man is the man in whose character there is established the tendency to respect the rights of others, and to subordinate thereto any conflicting desires of his own particular self—that he is the man who in this way realises the social self—we must yet allow for a progressive deepening and broadening of view concerning the nature of these rights. The permanent element in justice is the recognition of the moral personality of others. This recognition, when it has become ingrained in the good man's character, involves a recognition of their right to free activity, in so far as good ground has not been shown for its limitation ; and of their equality, unless there are special reasons for inequality. The interpretation and realisation of these rights is the problem of social progress. And our conception of justice is widened with the enlargement of our ideas as to what is involved in being a fellow-citizen, a fellow-man.

H

Into connexion with this view of justice, as respect for the rights of others, we may bring a number of other social virtues which are commonly regarded as independent :

1. Corresponding to the right acknowledged in every man to fair or equal treatment under the law, we have the judicial virtue of Impartiality.

2. Corresponding to his right to the goods or property which belong to him by law or by a moral right which we think should have the force of law, there is the virtue of Honesty.

3. Corresponding to his right to have promises kept and the truth told to him, we have the virtues of Promise-keeping and Veracity.

4. Corresponding to his right to have a due recognition of the benefits which he has conferred (even although these benefits may lose their moral worth if done for the sake of such a return) we have the virtue of Gratitude.

5. Corresponding to his right to freedom from interference, especially in those aspects of his life in which the individual is brought into relation with the ultimate meaning and purpose of reality, we have the virtue of Toleration.

CHAPTER VII

BENEVOLENCE

JUSTICE, as it has been explained, is a virtue of
wide compass, which has gradually widened its
extent with the enlargement of men's ideas of
citizenship and of manhood, and of the rights of a
citizen and of a man. The extension of the idea
of the rights of others may, indeed, be carried so
far as to make it difficult to distinguish justice from
benevolence. Both take in all mankind, and, as
we have seen, it is not easy to fix a limit to the
rights of manhood. Yet justice always seems to
contain an element of definite obligation, which
does not hold in the case of benevolence : a right
or claim on the one hand, and on the other a willingness to admit the claim, to respect the right. In
contrast with this, we may say that the virtue of
benevolence, like the quality of mercy, is not strained.
It does good beyond what can be required by any
definite claim, and there seems about it a certain
grace and freedom which the precise obligations of
justice tend to exclude. In some rare natures, however, this virtuous habit may be so powerful, and the
feeling of social unity may be so firmly established,

that the needs of other men may appeal with such strength and precision as to be indistinguishable from rights. " If citizens be friends," says Aristotle, " they have no need of justice ; but though they be just they need friendship or love also."

Benevolence, then, is the virtuous habit which leads a man to seek the good of others, even to the postponement of his private or particular interests, and to find his own in others' good. There is a true insight into the essence of this virtue of benevolence in Aristotle's view of friendship, where the good of one's friend is held to be identical with one's own. But the sentiment of friendship is so restricted in extent that it tends to transform the mutual love of two or three into an alliance against the rest of the world, and it also requires a certain correspondence of conditions and sentiments which prevents its wide extension. Benevolence, on the other hand, knows no such limits. In its highest form it is a love to all men, and to man as man.

The unemotional Jeremy Bentham once remarked —by way of explaining his own devotion to public objects, and reconciling it with his analysis of human motives—" I am a selfish man, as selfish as any man can be. But in me, somehow or other, so it happens, selfishness has taken the shape of benevolence." If we could admit this as a true account of a state of mind, prudence and benevolence would be for it the same both in motive and in the resultant conduct. At other times, especially when men are very closely connected with us—by family, or neighbourhood, or common profession—their need may seem to constitute a claim ; and in such cases—whenever we say that a particular person has a claim upon our benevolence—the distinction between justice and benevolence is being obliterated : so that for a perfect moral nature—a nature in which the good will is enlightened by perfect reason—we may surmise that benevolent action will be felt to appeal with the precision of justice, and that justice will be performed with the spontaneity of benevolence.

It is just this merging of the two into one which lends the element of grace to the most cultured and lovable moral natures.   Justice loses its rigidity ; benevolence its attitude of superiority ;   and the whole man seems dominated by a spirit of love which is at once a passion and a principle.

This leads to one of the difficulties connected with benevolence.   How is it possible (the question has been asked) to bring benevolence into line with the other virtues ?   They correspond to an attitude which may be regarded as a duty.   We may say to a man, " be sincere," " be just," " be pure," even " be brave."   But with what propriety can we say " thou shalt love " ?   Love, it has been said, is not

and never can be a command.   This view was taken
by Kant in his desire to purge morality of every
emotional element. John Stuart Mill, also, it may
be noted, never speaks of " benevolence," but always
of " beneficence " : as if the reference could only
be to a course of conduct which would promote
general happiness—never to a state of character
which would of itself lead to that result.   This view
has at least the merit of pointing to an important
distinction—the distinction between what may be
called the benevolence of sentiment and the benevolence of principle. The former has its root in the
feeling of sympathy, which may be described as the
instinctive basis of benevolence, as the feeling of
shame was said by Aristotle to be the instinctive
basis of temperance and the feeling of indignation
the instinctive basis of justice. But sympathy is
only the beginning of benevolence. If it remains
entirely in the region of feeling, it is apt to stimulate
action spasmodically and unequally. It may also
find as ready satisfaction in shutting the eyes to
suffering as in relieving it. We may imagine that
the priest and the Levite in the parable were men
of sympathetic emotions and could not bear to see
a fellow-creature in pain. They had, therefore,
to pass by on the other side. But they had not
attained the virtue of benevolence.

At the same time, the principle of benevolence, if

it remain a mere principle of reason, has failed to
spread itself over the whole nature and to work
itself out into a virtuous character. It leaves the
man untouched by any sense of unity with those
whom he benefits. The man who has merely the
principle of benevolence in him is apt to think
duty to humanity exhausted by an annual sub-
scription to the Charity Organisation Society.

Perhaps Kant's idea of benevolence—or rather
beneficence—may be not unfairly illustrated by
the portrait of Madame Beck drawn by Ch   otte
Brontë : " While devoid of sympathy, she had a
sufficiency of rational benevolence : she would give
in the readiest manner to people she had never
seen—rather, however, to classes than to individuals.
' Pour les pauvres,' she opened her purse freely—
against the poor man, as a rule, she kept it closed.
In philanthropic schemes for the benefit of society
at large she took a cheerful part ; no private sorrow
touched her : no force or mass of suffering con-
centrated in one heart had power to pierce hers.
Not the agony in Gethsemane, not the death on
Calvary, could have wrung from her eyes one tear."

The virtue which never reaches the reason is not
virtue but sentiment ; but the virtue which remains
in the reason and never leaves it, is equally imperfect. The continued will to do beneficent acts
becomes a voluntary habit and gives its tone to the

feelings ; and it is only when it has done so—when love has taken the place of law—that the character is truly benevolent.

A second disputed point arises in connexion with benevolence, and concerns the perennial question of the nature of the good. What is the nature of that good of other men which it is the benevolent man's formed volitional habit to seek ? If good, in the last analysis, could be resolved into a certain succession of pleasant feelings, then we might say that for others as for self, the end to be sought was happiness. It is, however, not on this ground only that the object of benevolence has been restricted to the promotion of happiness. Kant himself, the most consistent opponent of hedonistic morality, to whom the desire for pleasure (that is, one's own pleasure) was the typical expression of the maxim of the evil will,—Kant, nevertheless thought that our duty to our neighbours could be summed up in seeking their happiness or pleasure. His reason for this view was, however, very different from that which the utilitarian would give for the same doctrine. True goodness, he thought, lay in a state of will, in a will determined solely by the one moral motive, the reverence for moral law or goodness. It was too purely personal to be reached by any of those modifications of external conditions to which the actions of one man upon

another are restricted. Kant was indeed so concerned for the purity of morality that he may be
said to have banished it to another world, in which
sense cannot touch the springs of action and the
will is a timeless act. He thus makes inexplicable
two leading facts of morality—the moral nature
of society, and the moral progress made by the
individual.

If the individual can pass to higher stages of
moral attainment in his personal life—if moral
progress, that is, is a fact—it is because the impulsive and sensitive nature can become subdued
to and spiritualised by the moral law or moral
ideal ; because the good—that is, the good will—
can and does enter into those manifestations of
mental life in and through which a man stands
related to the world of nature and to other men.
The fact of moral progress, therefore, involves also
the connexion and mutual influence of the good will
with the perceptive and emotional life : through the
latter goodness is brought into a region which can
be touched and influenced by external conditions.

The good which social virtue seeks must, therefore, be of no meaner rank or lesser significance
than that which personal virtue contemplates as
its goal. If the attainment of many and varied
and lasting pleasures is a poor account of the moral
man's ideal for himself, it will be insufficient also

as a description of the good he can do to others.
Even Kant himself seems to recognise this when,
in spite of his own premises, he looks upon the
happiness of others which the good man seeks as
clearing from their path some of the obstacles to
virtue.

At the same time Kant's utterances on this point
—inaccurate as I think they are, and imperfectly
supported—may yet serve as a necessary caution
against what may be called the fanaticism of
benevolence. As a man's own moral progress is
slow and painful, and as " the native hue of resolution " is not only "sicklied o'er by the pale
cast of thought," but often sinks in the mire of
sense, or stumbles against the rocks of outward
circumstance—as it is only by repeated and constant
efforts, after many failures and doubtful battles,
that the good will attains its triumph and fashions
character in the likeness of its ideal—such but still
greater are the difficulties in the way of benevolent
activity producing goodness in others. For here
the influence is external ; and though it is never
perhaps without an internal effect—an effect on
character—that effect is hard to calculate. Alms-
giving may be misused, sympathy may be ridiculed
by its object ; so that demoralisation may be the
result of the most benevolent intentions. This is
indeed a commonplace. For in these days public

benevolence has become an art, and like other arts is in danger of passing into the hands of a special class of experts. It is well that it should be directed by all the knowledge which experience gives and by the insight which needs both tact and training. But the exercise of influence upon others is not a function of which an individual can rid himself and which he can lay on the shoulders of a selected class—like engineering or the practice of medicine. He cannot help exerting an influence deep or shallow, good or bad, upon his surroundings. This is at once the privilege and the duty which come from the moral solidarity of mankind. And the ideal benevolent man is he who recognises his moral unity with others, and strives, according to his opportunities, for them as well as for himself, to obtain the conditions and promote the activities of a worthy moral life.

A third question, which is not without difficulty, may be raised in conclusion. Who are the proper objects of benevolence ? To whom is it to be shown ?

We have already seen that, in the course of social and moral development, all the virtues gradually assume a wider sweep : courage extends beyond control of physical danger ; temperance reaches to the due ordering of other volitional systems than those of sensual desire. Similarly in the case of the

social virtues : justice recognises a widening circle
of rights ; and benevolence, also, makes universal
claims. Even a term for benevolence was unknown
to the classical moralists of Greece. The place
of the virtue was in part supplied by the exclusive
devotion of friendship, and in part by lesser virtues,
such as liberality, which really depend on benevolence. Citizens alone counted in the estimation of
Plato and Aristotle. Slaves and even aliens seemed
outside the sphere even of justice. But when the
city's independence was destroyed and the city
ceased to be the home and protector of the philosopher, he came to imagine a citizenship of the world
which—albeit in the barest outline—foreshadowed
modern philanthropic development. To the Stoics
the brotherhood of man, which they asserted, re-
mained a dream. And to us still, perhaps, it is only
a splendid vision, to which future ages may attain.
The practical difficulty of the benevolent man
arises when he is called upon to decide between the
competing claims of different social groups. Family
affection, patriotism, and philanthropy—to take
only the broadest and most general divisions—
often seem at issue with one another, and it is hard
to reconcile their conflicting interests ; perhaps
it is not always possible to do so in detail. The
simple rule, to do always what lies nearest, might
bind to narrow or party interests the powers that

were meant for mankind. On the other hand, to say that the larger group is always to have the preference, might play havoc with those closer bonds without which humanity itself must be driven from the path of progress. But perhaps two practical maxims may be given. One of these is that the extension of the sphere of benevolence should not be allowed to interfere with the intensive power and glow of the affection. The other is that devotion to our narrower surroundings should be accompanied by wider interests : the one will often inspire or enlighten the other. In making moral pocket-handkerchiefs for infant negroes in the West Indies, do not forget your station and its duties ; in cultivating your own garden, always remember that you are a citizen of the world.

CHAPTER VIII

RELIGION AND THE MORAL LIFE

THE question must now be asked whether the moral life, as it has been described in the preceding chapters, is complete in itself, or whether something more is needed for its perfection. If it is complete its parts must be so related as to form a unity. Further, as it is not a mere thought but a life, it needs power to overcome obstacles and to manifest its goodness. How are this unity and this power to be vindicated for the moral life ?

It is clear that it seeks unity and that it implies power in its manifestation. All the virtues bring system into human character and exhibit the control of the " lower " by the " higher " elements. The distinction of lower from higher has not been established, and cannot be established, by logical proof. It has been taken for granted that the spiritual life is better than the life of sense, and that the life of social service is better than selfishness. By applying this postulate a measure of unity has been shown to exist in the moral life, both in respect of the different manifestations of personal character and in respect of the competing claims of self and others. The moral attitude, however, is affected by the material upon which it works ; this modifies its scope at the same time that it gives a field for its exercise. Temperance, for example, is conditioned by the play of impulses and desires which are due to the animal nature of man and to his environment. Courage is built on a similar basis ; it has to restrain certain impulses and to regulate others. Justice and benevolence, in their exercise, are in obvious dependence upon social conditions. The good life is thus exhibited in many forms ; is it possible to state a single principle which will give unity to its variety ?

This principle of unity has been sought in two different directions : in reason, as the supreme factor in personal life ; and in the social order which conduct furthers or hinders. The former method is most prominent in Greek ethics. Wisdom was looked upon by the greatest thinkers as the source and measure of all kinds of goodness, as well as itself the supreme type of goodness. These thinkers have described the attributes of this intellectual life ; but always their description has tended to a dualism of a new kind. On the one hand, the philosopher only—if even he—can attain that pure vision of the l which is the source both of the reality and of the power of ordinary life. On the other hand, the great mass of men cannot see what he sees. They

may display the commonplace or civic virtues :
though they will do so only when they follow the
guidance of his reason and not of their own. Philosophers have shown various degrees of confidence
in the ability of this higher intellectual vision to
rationalise the grounds and issues of conduct. But,
even if their solution is adequate for their own lives,
it cannot be of any avail in the case of those by
whom the vision is unattainable ; and it leaves the
great majority of men to the lower morality of
following the bidding of the intellectual few.

This perhaps is the reason why modern writers,
as befits the citizens of a democratic state, favour
the other method and offer a social explanation
of morality. But this method also has its defects.
Society is nothing more than an organisation of
individual men which is capable of persisting through
the changes which birth and death make in its constituent members. Its life is not independent of
the persons who compose it ; nor has it value apart
from its contribution to the well-being of men.
To take the tendency to social vitality, or to social
order and progress, as the standard of goodness,
will give a working theory within certain limits.
These limits are set by the facts that society consists of and exists for men ; that the mere organisation is valueless apart from the persons organised ;
that forms of society are good or bad according to

the type of man they tend to produce and maintain ; and that the social order itself needs constant guidance and reform by moral ideas. It is true, conversely, that the individual is nothing apart from society ; but it does not follow from this that the latter sets the moral standard.

The difficulties connected with the conception of the social organism are avoided when the standard of morality is fixed by reference to the collection of individuals who make up society — or, rather, humanity. The form of utilitarianism advocated by John Stuart Mill may be taken as an example. According to this theory conduct is good or bad according to its effects upon the feelings of living beings. In spite of the shortness and uncertainty of individual life, the littleness of individual purposes, and the varieties of individual character, the utilitarian has endeavoured to find, in the whole mass of individuals, that permanence, elevation, and constancy which each unit lacks. Mill himself has left it on record that the " principle of utility " not only gave unity to his conception of things, but provided him with a religion. According to Sidgwick, the happiness of the " innumerable multitude of sentient beings, present and to come, seems an end that satisfies our imagination by its vastness, and sustains our resolution by its comparative security." And it is certain that many

I

noble lives have been lived without the light of
any further ideal. Yet it is only in default of a
final solution that it can have been put forward
as the last word. The ideal is impressive and
" comparatively secure "; but it fails to satisfy
the reason, and is apt to lose hold of the will. The
good or virtuous man is supposed to have this vast
and vague end in view. But the " innumerable
multitude of sentient beings present and to come "
are, after all, only a collection of transitory individuals—each with many failings, unworthy desires,
and imperfect ideals. Ministering to their pleasure
will not create the highest good; nor will a summa-
tion of their imperfections produce perfection.

The question, therefore, remains, Is any real
unity to be found in this multitude—any purpose
which the history of man may work out, or may be
slowly evolving ? If there is, and if we can in any
way apprehend it, there will inevitably arise an
attitude of mind towards this purpose, and in it
will be seen the true significance of life. On the
other hand, if no assertion at all can be made about
the matter—if our vision is limited to the play of
events—then conduct cannot be adapted to the
mere blank beyond. A completely indefinite possibility—so indefinite as to include a " nothing "
as one of its alternatives—puzzles the mind and
drys up the springs of action. " The world," said

Marcus Aurelius, " is either a welter of alternate combination and dispersion, or a unity of order and providence.   If the former, why crave to linger on in such a random medley and confusion ? why take thought for anything except the eventual ' dust to dust ' ? why vex myself ? do what I will, dispersion will overtake me.   But on the other alternative, I reverence, I stand stedfast, I find heart in the power that disposes all."   This latter attitude may be described as Religious Virtue.

The detail of life obscures its unity of purpose and makes the search for this unity difficult.   Incident is added to incident, as moment follows moment, each with a different experience, a new duty.   What has to be done varies with circumstances ; and these are infinite.   Moralists have commonly laid stress on the duties of man ; and, in so doing, they have given more or less precise directions for conduct, without bringing out the unity in its aim.   A man's duties are diverse ; but his performance of them may be slowly building up in him a consistent character.   It is in character that the unity to which moral action tends is most clearly expressed. Nevertheless the unity of the moral life is apt to remain far from perfect.   A man's character is developed in relation with the various institutions of his time—church and state, home and country,

I*

commerce and culture. We must look beyond these diverse institutions in order to find an objective unity which may be the archetype and architect of the subjective unity towards which the moral character tends.

A unity of this kind is supplied by the religious conception of the world. Of course it does not answer all the questions that may be put about the ultimate nature of reality or even about man's place in the universe. And the answers given will differ according to the intellectual and ethical characteristics of the religious belief. The religion may be tribal or national, and not universal. The higher powers which are the object of worship may be regarded as interested only in a particular people, or their rule may be supposed to be restricted to a certain territory. Even in such cases, however, a man feels himself to be in relation with a power which, within the limits of his imagination or sympathies, may be looked upon as ultimate. "What you see, yet cannot see over, is as good as infinite." Nor have religions always been ethical; they have their roots in other parts of man's nature as well as in the moral consciousness. Yet religion is never separated altogether from conduct. When it is said, as by Epicurus, that the gods take no concern in human affairs, religion ceases to exist. As men's conceptions of the godhead are purified, they enforce morality instead of conflicting with it ; as they are deepened, they tend to exhibit the varied content of morality in its connexion with a divine order.

The conception of a moral order of the world, and of this order as rooted in the nature of God, gives to the moral life the unity and power of which it stands in need.   It confirms the postulates of morality : the spiritual nature of God vindicates the supremacy of the spiritual factor in human life ;   the relation in which all men, as spiritual beings, stand to God gives meaning and validity to the idea of the brotherhood of men.   Both personal and social good are thus rooted in the same spiritual reality ;   and it overcomes their opposition because the spiritual reality, although it is more than either of them, is not a mere " beyond " but inspires them both.   In this way the religious conception of the world gives unity to the moral life.   And it also gives it power.   Moral enthusiasm can be fed only by the hope that effort is not in vain ;   and belief in God gives confidence that goodness will prevail.

The effect of religious faith is twofold.   It brings a new region of spiritual interests into man's life ; and it also affects his attitude to temporal concerns. The former effect widens the outlook of the moral life ;   the latter deepens its intensity.   But each has a danger of its own.   By bringing man into relation with the spiritual world new activities are introduced into his life. It is very easy to fit the whole sphere of religious observances into this scheme. Certain times of a man's life get set apart for the performance of what are called religious duties ; and the religious man comes to be regarded as the man by whom these duties are fully and punctually performed. Hence the tendency arises to distinguish religion from ordinary life in such a way as to lead to their separation ; and the religious life may be represented as something which can be led apart from the practice of the ordinary personal and social virtues. Every religion can produce examples of a high standard of religious observance combined with a poor performance of ordinary duties. The intense consciousness of the importance of the spiritual world may even lead to a disregard for the things of common life which easily lapses into immorality.

But religion and morality cannot for long be kept apart : unless, as in some creeds, God is confined to heaven and the world given over to the devil. The new spiritual interests act upon a man's inner attitude and thus affect the springs of conduct. If the object of faith be unworthy, the works of faith will diverge from the moral standard. But when there is faith in a God who is also goodness, the virtues of personal and social life will remain, only more securely based : active goodness will be intensified and the aspiration after an ideal perfection confirmed.

The faith on which religion is based has, as we have seen, a double effect. It is manifested in a life of its own in which man seeks and finds communion with God. It also supports and gives form to the moral life. Both influences were recognised by the theological moralists ; but there was often a tendency to exhibit them as if they were mutually independent, and simply to add on a new department of " theological virtues " to the virtues already recognised. The four traditional virtues of Plato's classification had been popularised by Cicero, and they were adapted to Christian teaching by Ambrose in the fourth century. Augustine, himself a pupil of Ambrose, supplemented these virtues by the apostolic triad of faith, hope, and charity or love : thus marking the difference between ordinary and religious virtue. Long afterwards this view came into connexion with a philosophical doctrine in which a deep and broad distinction was drawn between the natural and the supernatural. Human reason was regarded as competent in the former department ; but, for knowledge of the latter, man was held to depend on revelation. The same distinction was carried over into morality. There was a natural morality and a supernatural : the former

was the home of the traditional virtues, as described
by Plato or by Aristotle ; the latter consisted of the
virtues of faith, hope, and charity, which were com-
municated to man by divine grace. Thus the
kingdom of grace was regarded as a realm apart
from ordinary morality. Of the higher morality,
or morality of grace, love was the crown, faith the
condition ; and emphasis on its value led to de-
preciation of everything that was not of faith.
Long before the days of the schoolmen, Augustine
had said that true virtue was impossible without true
religion ; and his influence led to the description of
the virtues of the heathen as " splendid vices." He
failed to do justice to the moral consciousness that
follows the good simply because it sees it to be good,
and without thought of anything beyond. The
same narrow view outlasted the times of the schoolmen. " I give no alms," said Sir Thomas Browne,
" to satisfy the hunger of my brother, but to fulfil
and accomplish the will and command of my God " ;
and, in so saying, forgot the gospel he followed,
which makes the love of one's brother come first
and prepare the way for the love of God. The view
with which these statements are connected mistakes
the true bearing of religion upon morality. Religion
does not supplant ordinary morality and substitute
something else ; but it deepens a man's insight into
what is good, and renders it support.

It is of the essence of the religious attitude, as formed by Christianity, that the moral law and moral ideals are regarded as belonging to the nature of God and as in some way realised in His perfection.   The performance of one's duties as divine commands—which Kant regarded as the fundamental element in religion—is not rightly interpreted as mere obedience to a supreme legislator. It implies the recognition of the divine will as also the highest goodness, and of morality, therefore, as attaining its perfection in likeness to God.

The religious attitude influences the whole content of morality : gives it form, as has been already said.   It also accentuates certain qualities in the moral life which, apart from religion, would not receive the same prominence.   Two of these qualities call for some remark.

Humility is commonly regarded as characteristic of Christian morality in contrast with the classical or pagan ideal of what was admirable in man.   And, on the whole, this view is correct.   Yet Greek ethics, at any rate, is not altogether silent on the point.   Insolence or overweening conceit was looked upon as a sin which the gods would punish.   It was more than a sin ; it was an offence against good taste :   an excess which went beyond the limits of due and moderate self-estimate.   And it was condemned in small things as in great ; witness

Aristotle's condemnation of boastfulness as a vicious extreme hurtful to the amenities of social intercourse. But the question may be asked, Is not humility the opposite extreme, and as far removed from virtue ?

On this question there certainly seems to be a considerable divergence between the Greek and the Christian estimates : though the divergence is not so great as it is sometimes represented as being. Critics of Christian morality, from early times to the present, have been in the habit of contrasting the cringing attitude of the Christian saint, who wallows in the mire in presence both of God and of man, with the noble self-assertion and virile virtues of the Greek and Roman citizens. The opposition is unduly accentuated. As a social attitude the Christian virtue might perhaps be better described, in Aristotelian fashion, as a mean between two familiar but vicious extremes—that of abject self-abasement and that of spiritual arrogance. As an attitude towards God it expresses a man's consciousness both of the perfection of his ideal and of the deficiency of his own performance. Further defined, it becomes a consciousness of sin. Now this attitude *is* different from the pagan virtue either of the antique model or of its modern copy. The difference is due to the ideal of realised goodness with which a man compares himself. The moral element

was not usually strong in ancient pagan conceptions
of ultimate reality.   From some modern conceptions
it is entirely absent ; and the modern consciousness
seeks an historical explanation of its own imperfections which is fitted to offend personal vanity as
little as possible.

It is quite true, however, that humility lies close
to many grave defects of character.   It is an easy
virtue — or no virtue at all—for the weak of will
and lovers of repose.   But true humility, which
does not pride itself unduly about what has
been done, does not imply the poverty of spirit
which leads a man so to distrust his powers
that he becomes incapable of effective action.
In the man of earnest purpose, who knows his
strength and uses it to carry out his plans, but
refrains from proclaiming his own merits and admits
the merits of others, we find the better manifestation of humility, and this attitude finds outward
expression in courteous social bearing.

Reverence is the counterpart of humility in
Christian morals.   Reverence for the ideal—for the
law, as Kant puts it—inevitably humbles the man
who is conscious of its perfection and of his own
defects.   But humility is only the negative aspect
of this consciousness—the side of it which represses
pride and claim to merit on the part of the individual.
There is also a positive aspect.   Reverence for the

ideal involves consciousness of it and a certain community with it. Man bows before its perfection ; but he also recognises himself as the bearer of morality and as charged with its realisation. The same consciousness which may lead him to call himself an unprofitable servant shows him the dignity of his moral calling. He recognises that his worth is not to be measured merely by what he does but also by what he is capable of doing ; and this consciousness of the capacity for goodness has some power in working out its own realisation. On the other hand, reverence sometimes accentuates the feeling of humility. The man who recognises most fully the dignity of other men is often most alive to his own shortcomings. His reverence for the ideal produces a deeper sense of the distance which separates it from his own performance : just as the man who has done most to widen knowledge may think his discoveries of small account compared with the realms of truth still unknown.

NOTES

PAGE

2. Pascal, *Pensées et Opuscules*, ed. Brunschvigg, 5th edit., 1909, p. 465.
3. Macaulay, *Essay on Machiavelli.*
4. Westermarck, *Origin and Development of the Moral Ideas*, I. 118.
7. Westermarck, *op. cit.*, II. 742-3.
13. Compare the conception of καλοκαγαθία, Aristotle, *Ethics*, IV. iii. 16 ; X. ix. 3.
14. For the term Physical Virtue, see Aristotle, *Ethics*, VII. viii. 4 ; for Intellectual Virtue, see also Aristotle, *Ethics*, I. xiii. 20, and Book VI.
16. See Plato, *Republic*, Book IV., especially pp. 441-4.
19. " Reason alone can never produce any action, or give rise to volition. . . . Reason is, and ought only to be the slave of the passions, and can never pretend to any other office than to serve and obey them."—Hume, *Treatise of Human Nature*, II. iii. 3.
30. Jowett, *Dialogues of Plato*, 2nd edit., I. 3.
36. Leslie Stephen, *Life of Sir J. F. Stephen*, p. 61. The reference is to their father Sir James Stephen.
36. W. James, *Principles of Psychology* (1890), I. 126. The sentences are repeated in his *Talks to Teachers on Psychology* (1899), p. 75.
39. Compare Spinoza, *Ethics*, iv. 47.
41. The conception of a " universe of desire " was introduced into ethics by Prof. J. S. Mackenzie, *Manual of Ethics* (1893), pp. 74-6.
43. T. H. Green, *Prolegomena to Ethics* (1883), p. 291.

PAGE

47. Boswell, *Life of Samuel Johnson*, chap. 44.

48. Plato, *Laws*, Book XII. p. 965 E.

49. Aristotle, *Ethics*, III. vi. 10.

51. R. L. Stevenson, *Catriona*, chap. 13.

54. Plato, *Laws*, Book I. p. 649.

56. " I am afraid there is no other way of ascertaining the truth but by persecution on the one hand, and enduring it on the other." —Boswell's *Life of Johnson*, chap. 27.

56. Shaftesbury, *Letter concerning Enthusiasm*, § 3, *Characteristics*, Vol. I.

60. *Von Moltke as a Correspondent*, tr. M. Herms; quoted by Bodley, *France*, II., 367n.

60. W. Bagehot, *Physics and Politics*, p. 47.

66. R. L. Stevenson, *Virginibus Puerisque*, p. 65.

67. B. Bosanquet, *Companion to Plato's Republic* (1895), p. 227.

69. A. Birrell, *Obiter Dicta* (1884), Essay on " Truth-hunting."

71. Compare the condemnation of hired labour and retail trade, *e.g.*, in Cicero, *De Officiis*, i. 42.

72. Thackeray, *Pendennis*, chap. 36.

73. Boswell's *Life of Johnson*, chap. 30.

73. Bax, *Religion of Socialism*, p. 94.

74. Aristotle, *Ethics*, IV. iii.

76. J. S. Nicholson, *Economic Journal*, VII. 543.

78. Butler, *Analogy*, Diss. ii., " On the Nature of Virtue," *Works* (1849), pp. 317, 319.

79. Kant, *Metaphysische Anfangsgründe der Tugendlehre*, introd. § 4 ; *Grundlegung zur Metaphysik der Sitten*, Part I. (Kant's *Critique of Practical Reason and other Works*, translated by T. K. Abbott, 3rd edit., pp. 296, 10-11.)

81. Bax, *Religion of Socialism*, p. 95.

82. Plato, *Phædrus*, p. 257 (Jowett's translation).

82. Jane Austen, *Persuasion*, chap. 1.

90. Aristotle, *Ethics*, II. vii. 14-15.

91. Cp. J. A. Stewart, *Notes on the Nicomachean Ethics of Aristotle*, I. 214.

PAGE

96. Cp. Sidgwick, *Methods of Ethics*, Book III. chap 5.

103. Kant, *Metaphysische Anfangsgründe der Rechtslehre* (*Werke*, ed. Hartenstein, VII. 27); Spencer, *Principles of Ethics*, Part IV., " Justice," § 27.

116. Aristotle, *Ethics*, VIII. i. 4.

116. Bentham, *Works*, XI. 95.

119. C. Brontë, *Villette*, chap. 8.

125. Cp. Dickens, *Pickwick*, chap. 27; Voltaire, *Candide*, concluding sentence.

129. J. S. Mill, *Autobiography*, pp. 66-7.

129. Sidgwick, *Methods of Ethics*, 6th edit., p. 404.

131. Marcus Aurelius Antoninus *To Himself*, vi. 10 (Rendall's translation, 1898, p. 70).

132. Carlyle, *Sartor Resartus*, ii. 1.

136. Augustine, *De civitate Dei*, xix. 25.

136. Sir T. Browne, *Religio medici*, ii. 2.

SUPPLEMENTARY NOTE.—For further study of the topics discussed in the preceding chapters the reader is referred to Sidgwick's *Methods of Ethics*, Book III.; T. H. Green's *Prolegomena to Ethics*, Books III. and IV.; and Paulsen's *System of Ethics*, Book III. He will also find much matter bearing on the subject, as well as a guide to ethical questions and ethical literature generally, in any one of the following introductory treatises:—J. H. Muirhead, *Elements of Ethics*; J. S. Mackenzie, *Manual of Ethics*; J. Seth, *A Study of Ethical Principles*; J. Dewey and J. H. Tufts, *Ethics*.

INDEX

Veracity, 114
Virtue, 2, 21
—— cardinal, 26 *f.*, 70
—— —— classification of, 25
—— intellectual, 16 *f.*, 62 *f.*
—— personal and social, 22 *f.*, 86 *f.*
—— natural, 14 *f.*
—— religious, 131

—— theological, 24, 135
Virtus, 47

Westermarck, E., 4, 6
Will, 11 *f.*
—— and reason, 17 *f.*
—— and the good, 65
Wisdom, 62 *f.*, 127

www.ingramcontent.com/pod-product-compliance
Ingram Content Group UK Ltd.
Pitfield, Milton Keynes, MK11 3LW, UK
UKHW042145280225
455719UK00001B/123